TRAVELS WITH CHARLIZE
IN SEARCH OF LIVING ALONE

David R. Gross

BOOK PUBLISHERS NETWORK
Changing the World One Book at a Time

Book Publishers Network
P.O. Box 2256
Bothell • WA • 98041
PH • 425-483-3040
www.bookpublishersnetwork.com

10 9 8 7 6 5 4 3 2 1

Printed in the United States of America

LCCN 2014955585
ISBN   978-1-940598-54-3

Editor: Julie Scandora
Cover designer: Laura Zugzda
Typographer: Melissa Vail Coffman

DEDICATION

*To Rosalie, I think of you and miss you everyday
and will do so for the rest of my life.*

ACKNOWLEDGEMENTS

As with any piece of worthwhile writing the finished product is excruciatingly dependent upon the input of experts. I need to thank Carolyn Acheson who suggested I put together my blogs into a book and guided me through the initial efforts. Thanks to Julie Scandora for her expert editorial help, Melissa Coffman for the layout and formatting, Laura Zugzda for the cover design and Sheryn Hara of the Book Publishers Network for her encouragement and sage advice.

PROLOGUE

I've BEEN REREADING JOHN STEINBECK's *Travels with Charley: In Search of America*, as well as two of his other works I somehow missed—*The Winter of Our Discontent* and *The Log from the Sea of Cortez*. Steinbeck's Charley was a standard French poodle with an American name. My Charlize is a German shepherd with a French name. Steinbeck was on a mission to discover the America of his day and his place in it. After almost fifty-three years of marriage, I'm on a mission to discover how to live without Rosalie, the love of my life.

Charlize—pronounced Charley—is a rescue dog, my third German shepherd. She's about three years old, and we hooked up less than two weeks after Rosalie's passing. After applying online to Seattle's German shepherd rescue organization, I was interviewed and approved. Charlize came with a different name, but having decided to mimic Steinbeck's travels, I renamed her. All we know about Charlize's history is that she came from a shelter in Utah because she still had the tags from that shelter. I do know that we're two injured beings who need to support each other.

I

In the Beginning

HOLDING ROSALIE CLOSE, I cradled her head in my arms as she died. On the twenty-third of April, we would have celebrated fifty-three years of marriage. I'm coping—sort of.

A week before she died, we were sitting next to each other on our recliners. We weren't paying attention to the endless commercials that incessantly interrupted David Letterman who was failing to interest us.

"Well," she said, pulling out the nasal tube that was flowing oxygen into her nostrils, "pretty soon you'll be able to get a dog."

Bear, our previous German shepherd, had died six years previously, and we didn't get another dog. That was the only time in my life that I can remember being dog-less, but Rosalie had developed balance problems—the aftermath of a viral encephalopathy and a brain biopsy, and we were worried that she would trip or fall over a dog. She knew I missed having a dog, and her out-of-the-blue statement was typical of her dark sense of humor.

"Stop talking nonsense," I responded.

Throughout our last six months together, I prayed that the end would be fast and with as little pain and discomfort as possible. Her diagnosis of stage-four lung cancer came on January 4, 2012, after we noticed she had trouble breathing after only mild exercise. This was troubling because she routinely logged eleven to fourteen miles in fifty or sixty minutes on our stationary bike, burning more than three hundred calories four or five times a week.

Her oncologist at the Seattle Cancer Care Alliance explained that the average statistics for her diagnosis were survival of three to six months. As a scientist, I was (and still am) convinced that the brain can heal any disease of the body if only we can figure out how to invoke the necessary killer cells, immunological responses, or whatever other body defense mechanisms are necessary by sending the correct messages from the brain. So I nagged Rosalie with all the determination I could muster about the power of positive thinking and prayer. I encouraged her to visualize her tumors and direct her body defense mechanisms to kill those nasty, unwanted, unwarranted growths.

With her typical quiet determination, Rosalie made it to six months, then eight, then ten and counting. She tired easily but appeared normal to everyone except me. A very private person, she didn't want friends, or especially acquaintances, to know that she was seriously ill. Our two sons knew, but they humored her pretending this was just a minor inconvenience to be overcome.

In mid-December, she needed supplemental oxygen, and on December 27, the oncologist suggested home hospice care. The hospice people showed up and enrolled her on January 2. Because of the holidays, the people from the hospice were unable to supply the oral morphine she needed to remain comfortable. She soldiered through with the painkillers and other medications we had on hand. She didn't complain. Finally, on January 3, we were supplied and instructed. We were trying to adjust to the next stage of the experience.

• • •

My first German shepherd was named Mister. He and I hooked up during the summer before my second year in veterinary school. His AKC name was Docdave's Mister Lucky Streak. I had won a hundred dollars in a poker game and went out the next morning to spend the winnings before I could lose them back. When I arrived at the breeder's, the ball of fur waddled over, sat on my foot, and looked up at me as if to say, "Well, boss, aren't we going home?"

During the school year, Mister's home was the back seat of my car. Before I met Rosalie, all the girls I dated made a big fuss over him, but he was a regal sort and mostly ignored them. On my first date with Rosalie, when I held the car door open for her, Mister was all over her. She gave him a perfunctory pat on the head, but he wouldn't leave her alone. He kept nuzzling her, pushing his head under her arm and hand, begging to be petted. I twisted in the seat, ordered him to sit down and stay—and noticed that he had an erection. I decided then and there not to ignore his intuition. It wasn't long until I came to the realization that I agreed totally with him!

• • •

The first two days after Charlize moved in with me, she was apprehensive and distraught, but since then, she's calm and protective, and we've bonded. I keep her with me all the time. She's housebroken and vehicle-broken and fetches tennis balls like a retriever. This is good exercise for her, and it saves my gimpy left ankle.

Here is Charlize, a handsome young lady, posing for the camera.

2

ON THE ROAD

THE FRUSTRATIONS OF THE LAST FOUR DAYS before my obsessively determined departure date were over. Who would believe that a newly single adult male and his dog could experience so many last-minute problems in trying to get out of town? But all came together, and Charlize and I, comfortable in Old Blue and pulling the Frog, were the last to board the Edmonds-Kingston ferry on the first of March.

Old Blue was the 2012 Dodge Ram 1500 in charge of making our journey possible. The Frog was my brand-new—albeit slightly crowded with both of us in attendance—camping trailer. Frog pulled like a dream, sticking close to Old Blue's tail.

The purpose of this road trip was to try to figure out what I should do with my remaining years and how to do it. I'm seventy-six years old, and for more than fifty-two of those years, I was married to the only girl I ever truly loved. I'm not accustomed to making decisions on my own. Charlize is a good listener but doesn't contribute much, except enthusiasm, to the decision-making process.

I decided to start out on familiar roads, roads that Rosalie and I had taken previously to Port Townsend, Sequim, and Port Angeles, Washington. Once Charlize and I were west of Port Angeles, we were in new territory. We took a short detour to see what destruction of the dam had wrought to the Elwha River, now flowing gray with silt and debris. I hadn't seen it prior to the return to a more natural state. Undoing the well-meant but ultimately destructive "improvements" to Mother Nature might take some time.

Deciding at the last moment to forego the civilized amenities of an RV park in Forks, we pressed on to the Kalaloch Campground. My Senior Pass to all the national parks and recreational lands bought a night for only seven dollars. There are a few advantages to being a senior!

We parked about ten feet from a split-rail fence. Just beyond the fence was a brush-covered drop-off, twenty-five or so yards above the beach. Gentle breakers provided a soothing, monotonous background to a day of calm healing. Finally, I was away from the terrible reminders of our house, Rosalie's things, and a previous life. Charlize was keeping close watch on me. She seemed to need respite from her previous life as much as I did.

Split rail fence, the ocean beyond.

Relentless waves were working their way onto the sand with a sound similar to a busy highway. In Mexico, the lack of synchronization of the incoming waves could be described as *a vez en cuando* (from time to time). The saying conveys inevitability, the inability of any human to change events.

Half of the Kalaloch Campground was closed, the road barred by a red-and-white-striped railroad-crossing-type gate. I suppose only those persons seeking solitude find their way to that place, normally rain soaked but now dry. The open half had thirty-some camping spots, but only seven were occupied. Not a single person greeted us. Everyone was holed up in his or her camper.

That night, actually about four o'clock in the morning, I woke up thinking about Rosalie's last minutes, and I started crying. Charlize immediately came over and stuck her nose under my arm, determined to comfort me. It worked.

3

THE KALALOCH CAMPGROUND

IN THE FIFTIES, my family did a lot of car camping with a luggage
trailer and big umbrella tent—the only sort of vacation my folks
could afford. Much later, our sons and I backpacked and made many
momentous decisions about their lives while we sat freezing on a moun-
taintop. Rosalie wasn't much interested in camping, preferring modern
plumbing. Now, Charlize and I were the campers.

Saturday morning at six o'clock, Charlize and I walked the Kalaloch
Campground in the dark. Well, it wasn't really dark. A half-moon was
out—bright, but not as bright as the moon I remember from my growing up in Phoenix, long before that place became the bloated sprawl
in the desert that it is today. The winter moon of the desert, the desert
that I remember, was bright enough to read by—or maybe my eyes
were young enough to see by.

Gray dawn near the Kalaloch Campground.

During the night, a sheet of ice had formed on Old Blue's windows. The moon, still bright before dawn, illuminated the stark silhouettes of Douglas fir, various pines, Sitka spruce, and western red cedar, all in stark relief. Their trunks bent slightly east, toward the Olympics. Their tops, sheared by high winds blowing in from the ocean, pointed at the mountains.

Charlize and I ate our breakfasts—she, her kibble mixed with a dash of chicken bouillon; I, coffee and instant oatmeal. Then I cleaned up with her close supervision to make certain everything was done properly. We were ready to leave before seven o'clock. All the other RVs were still dark, their occupants sleeping in. We hadn't seen a soul during our time there.

On the road again, Charlize barked when a highway construction flagman approached Old Blue to kibitz about Frog. This wasn't that incessant barking typical of some dogs, just one sharp warning to let that guy know she was on duty. I guess she decided that I belong to her and am in need of both comforting and protection.

4

DAY-TWO MUSINGS

DAY TWO ACTUALLY STARTED at five o'clock in the morning. I'm still unable to sleep more than two or three hours at a time with hours of being awake in-between. Not unusual, I'm told, for this stage of grief. Charlize and I got away early enough for me to eat a second too-big breakfast at the Quinault Lodge on the edge of Lake Quinault. I ordered sausage and eggs, over easy, with breakfast potatoes, toast, and coffee.

I decided that the meal would be the last big breakfast for me. I was going to change my eating habits, at least during my journey of discovery. We'll see how that plays out once I'm home. My plan was to eat oatmeal for breakfast, eat a big meal at noon, usually in a restaurant, and then just a light dinner, some soup or an omelet or maybe a sandwich.

After my big breakfast, I hobbled with my arthritic left ankle over the half-mile-long nature trail, a sign-guided tour of a small corner of the Quinault Rain Forest. Charlize did at least two miles, up and back, side-to-side, a myriad of new and unusual smells to catalogue. I wonder if she remembers the odors or if each time she smells something it is a whole new experience.

Trail through the Quinault Rain Forest, Charlize leading the way.

We stopped for a late lunch at South Bend, Washington, on Route 101, only four miles from Raymond. I had spotted a chef in front of his restaurant grilling fresh oysters over a wood fire and couldn't resist. I watched as the oysters cooked in cedar smoke at least twelve inches from the flames while being basted with the chef's secret marinade.

Inside, I collaborated with a nice lady and her husband, who were sitting at an adjoining table, to try to identify the ingredients of the marinade. We decided it contained lots of fresh, coarsely chopped garlic, green onions, fresh green herbs, maybe basil or parsley or something else, maybe a combination, in a vinegar base, probably a malted vinegar, not Balsamic. We probably left out or incorrectly identified some of the ingredients, but our chef wasn't giving anything away, and he most certainly didn't share proportions.

About four o'clock in the afternoon, Charlize and I arrived at the Lewis and Clark National and State Historical Parks. Many believe that Clark named the location—the first true sighting of the Pacific—Cape Disappointment because of the lousy weather the corps endured for several days running. However, the name appears on maps made by Captain Vancouver a year before the Corps of Discovery started its journey, and John Meares, an English fur trader, named that location in 1788.

The campground is owned and operated by the state of Washington. Frog was all set up with electrical power and fresh water but no Wi-Fi, no cell phone service, and no TV. Still roughing it.

Charlize on the black sand beach, maybe near the spot where the Corps of Discovery viewed the Pacific Ocean for the first time.

I played fetch with Charlize on the beach for half an hour, but I didn't throw her tennis ball too far out into the surf, as it appeared to have a strong undertow. The dog is insatiable, fetching with the enthusiasm of a retriever. When she was panting hard, we sat on the wet sand and watched the sun go down. I mused about sitting on the same black sand that Lewis and Clark had walked. I wondered if Lewis threw a stick into the surf for his Newfoundland dog, named Seaman, to retrieve.

5

RELIVING LEWIS AND CLARK

TRUE TO MY OBSESSIVE, head-down, and push-until-the-task-is-complete nature before Charlize and I embarked on the odyssey, I had sat at my computer and printed out Google maps for nine days of travel. I managed to ignore all that planning by stopping to take in anything that caught my interest. Charlize was happy just to be participating.

I found special joy chatting with the helpful folks handing out pamphlets, maps, and advice at small-town chamber of commerce information offices. Any simple question I asked about the history of their community evoked enthusiastic replies. They obviously derived considerable pleasure from my interest in their home town. Rosalie and I had moved around so much during our fifty-two years of marriage that we had never seemed to form a real sense of belonging with any of the places we lived. They were all temporary stops in our life together. Now I find I am a little jealous of people who have lived their life in one locale and are happy about it.

Before leaving Sunday morning, Charlize and I walked portions of the Discovery Trail and then tacked on a rather difficult mile or so with me struggling on my gimpy ankle up and down the steep trail to the North Head Lighthouse. Just a few years ago, those trails would have been a piece of cake. We were just killing time until the interpretive center opened at ten, but we had been up since five-thirty so we had a lot of time to kill.

The view from the top of the Discovery Trail.

At the interpretive center, Charlize had to stay tied up outside, but the volunteer lady at the front desk told me as I left that Charlize had greeted each new visitor by barking while wagging her tail. The lady said Charlize appeared to be happy to be petted by those brave enough to try. Charlize has a classical German shepherd's look but is small, only sixty-five pounds; most females weigh over seventy-five.

I have devoured many books, including the various edited versions of the captains' journals dealing with the great adventure of the Corps of Discovery. The interpretive center was well done with some nice period artifacts. Well worth the time and effort, but I didn't learn anything new.

I was still having trouble sleeping through the night. That night, I had fallen asleep quickly but woke up about three o'clock. Previously when I got up during the night, Charlize was on the floor next to my bed. That morning she wasn't. Inside Frog, the back end of the camper consists of a U-shaped bench around a small table. The table can be lowered, and the back cushions used to make a double bed. I turned on a light and saw her peeking out from the starboard side bench obviously apprehensive about being on the furniture. I told her she was a good girl and could use the bench for a bed. It kept me from tripping over her when I got up during the night. However, during the day, she was not allowed on it. She seemed to adjust to my weird rules.

We visited the reconstructed Fort Clatsop, south of the Columbia, where the Corps of Discovery spent a miserable winter. Even in nice weather, it was easy to imagine how uncomfortable they must have been.

We were back on 101, the Pacific Coast Scenic Byway, about one in the afternoon.

6

AHEAD OF SCHEDULE, ARE WE HAVING FUN YET?

THE NEXT NIGHT, we stayed in a KOA campground in Lincoln City, Oregon. The place had all the amenities, the people that ran it were nice, and the facilities were average. Frog's hot water heater didn't work, nor did the combination radio, TV, and DVD player. Frustrating.

Charlize obviously decided I belong to her and am in need of both comforting and protection. About four o'clock in the morning, I again woke up thinking about Rosalie's last minutes and started crying. Charlize jumped off her bench and came over to stick her nose under my arm, determined to comfort me. It worked.

After an hour or so, unable to go back to sleep, I fed Charlize, ate my quick breakfast of instant oatmeal and a cup of coffee, and then disconnected everything and continued our journey until stopping at an RV sales, service, and parts store in Newport, Oregon. I was determined to find out why Frog's water heater wasn't working. It turned out to be just a case of my ignorance. I knew there were two switches for the heater but learned the one accessible from outside Frog controls the propane gas flow. Another switch, inside, controls the electricity for the starter. While Frog is in use, I am supposed to leave the gas switch on. When I am ready for hot water, I have to turn on the electrical switch inside under the sink. When the latter switch is turned on, a red light goes on that says "reset."

Before this revelation, I thought something was wrong and spent three days reading the owner's manual and trying to figure out how to reset the thing. It cost me twenty bucks to find out I was just too impatient. After a while, the burner ignites, and the red light goes off. I had yet to find the manual for the DVD-TV-radio device and figure out why I couldn't make that work. By the time the trip was over, I expected to be a qualified RV mechanic.

On the coast highway, we stopped many times just to contemplate and stare at the ocean. Wave follows wave, long lines separated by time and space. Some break over, spilling white turbulence, before arriving at the rocks. Others crash against those stalwarts. Not all the huge rocks constitute the shoreline cliffs. Some stand out in the Pacific as outposts, forward observers. They are battered, ceaselessly pummeled, fighting against the inevitability of erosion. Some of these outposts defied reason. From them sprouted one, sometimes more, ridiculously determined evergreen trees. I have no idea what kind of trees they were. Probably, as my ten-year-old granddaughter often advises, I can Google it, but where's the fun in that?

The Pacific Ocean, anything but pacific.

7

NAMING VEHICLES

THE FIRST AUTOMOBILE I DROVE was a 1940 Chevy two-door sedan. My folks allowed me to drive it when I was sixteen and a junior in high school. It wasn't much of a car in 1953. My dad had bought it new and then driven it from Cleveland, Ohio, to Phoenix, Arizona, in 1944 at forty-five miles an hour on rationed gas and retread tires. By the time I drove it, the running boards and rear fenders had rusted and fallen off. The upholstery was worn and torn, so my mom made slipcovers in a variety of patterns and colors from upholstery fabric samples. I didn't care—I was thrilled to have wheels and the freedom that came with them.

Since then, I've owned at least seventeen vehicles. After I built my own veterinary practice during the 1960s, I traded vehicles every couple of years. If only all the money I spent purchasing and operating those cars and trucks was still in my pocket! Of course, all those vehicle purchases served a purpose at the time—or at least I thought they did.

Rosalie and I started naming vehicles at some point, but I can't remember why. The first name I remember was a 1985 Chevy S-10 pickup. The truck always had problems with the fuel injection and oxygen detector systems, so it was named "Lurch" for obvious reasons. In 1997, Rosalie decided she would be most comfortable getting in and out of and driving a minivan. That gray Dodge Caravan was the first car with her name on the title as the owner. She called it "Gray Baby" but rarely put more than six or eight thousand miles a year on it.

In 2011, we decided to buy our last vehicle prior to being too old to drive anymore. This time, we went upscale and acquired a new Chrysler Town and Country, albeit the previous year's model. Rosalie called this one "Gray Baby Too." I was driving a 2002 Toyota Tundra 4X4, known as the "Green Monster Truck."

After Rosalie passed away, I couldn't get into Gray Baby Too without crying, so I traded her and the green monster truck for Old Blue. This time, Charlize participated in the vehicle choice and concurred with the naming.

Here is Old Blue, Frog in tow, resting while I check out a tourist trap near Big Sur.

Naming vehicles may seem a little weird, but at least Charlize and I didn't conjure up a literary reference that few people would recognize today. Steinbeck's truck was named Rocinante, the same as Don Quixote's horse.

8

SHAKEDOWN CRUISE

THE TRUE SHAKEDOWN CRUISE for Frog started after Charlize and I left Oregon. We stopped at the chamber of commerce information office in Crescent City, California, and a helpful man at the desk insisted that we see the Jedediah Smith Redwoods State Park. I have an unquenchable thirst for anything having to do with the mountain man era, so I decided this was something Charlize and I should do. Jedediah Smith was a giant among mountain men.

"You don't have to go back to the intersection of 101 and 197 to get there," the guy told me. "You can take this back road in." He showed me the roads on a map and gave me the map. I hate to backtrack.

"It's about fifteen miles of gravel, but you can make it with your truck. It's a four-by-four isn't it?"

"Yeah ... sounds good. We'll give it a try," I replied.

Well, it wasn't a gravel road. It was a single lane of mud and dirt with huge, water-filled potholes and sixteen miles of curves, switchbacks, up and down and around and weaving through massive redwood trees that refused to move out of our way.

About five miles in, a friendly lady park ranger sitting in her jeep waved us to a stop and said, "There's a sign back there that says 'trailers not advised.'"

"Whoops," I responded. "Guess I was too busy trying to keep this rig on the road and didn't see it. Anyplace near where I can turn this outfit around?"

She looked long and hard at Old Blue and Frog, almost forty feet of combined length and shook her head.

"Don't think so. You best take it slow and easy."

"If I get stuck or wrecked, do I call 911?"

"No use. No cell phone service out here. We'll find you … eventually." She smiled sweetly.

"Brilliant … OK … Hope I don't see you again today."

She smiled again. "Hope not."

We made it, but everything bounced out of the cabinet above the stove and out of the netted shelf over the sink. All the contents of the drawers were rearranged, but no permanent damage was done, and all the various systems continued to function.

Charlize and I both needed a break after a
bumpy ride through the redwoods.

The inside of Frog was efficient, similar to a sailboat, capable of accommodating a couple of people comfortably. The door was located on the passenger side of Old Blue, in front of the trailer's wheels. A handrail folded back against the cabin, and a pullout stair enabled me to climb in, albeit clumsily with my bad ankle.

Through the door to the immediate right was an odd-sized bed, forty-four inches wide and seventy-two inches long, wider than a twin bed but narrower than a double. The length filled the entire six-foot width of Frog, so at more than six feet two inches, I slept on the diagonal. Originally there were built-in bunk beds with no more than eighteen inches between them. Before I bought Frog, I asked the dealer to remove the top bunk, which he did. The mattress now was directly atop a plywood platform with some rather inaccessible storage underneath. The mattress had to be taken off to make the bed. I decided that when I got home I would make some renovations to make the bed and storage under it more accessible and useful.

To the immediate left through the door was the kitchen cabinet. It housed a two-burner LP gas stovetop and a small sink. There were two overhead cabinets, another cabinet under the stove, and three drawers under the sink. Across a two-foot space from the stovetop was the head containing a very small sink, a shower, and a toilet, all plastic, all waterproof, all functional—but a tight fit for a person as big as I am. Across the same small space from the sink there was an eye-level cabinet that housed a combination microwave/convection oven and a lot of Frog's mechanical equipment, including the hot-water heater, the furnace, the clean-water tank, and more.

At the back end of the cabin was that U-shaped bench I told you about with a small table. The table could be lowered, and the back cushions of the bench used to make another, odd-sized bed for two small people or for one normal-sized person. Charlize was careful to keep clear of me and avoided getting stepped on. It was cramped but cozy.

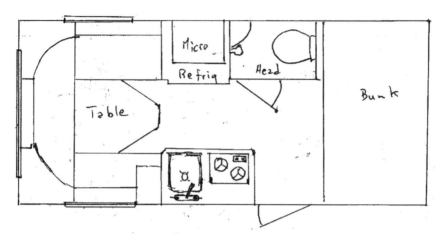

My rough sketch of Frog's interior.

Our home on the road was significantly larger than John Stein-beck's, although he is reported as having spent more times in upscale motels and hotels than in his pickup-mounted camper. Great writing makes up for a few white lies.

9

OLD FRIENDS ARE THE BEST

WE STOPPED IN SALINAS and spent the afternoon and evening with a veterinary school classmate, Gary, and his significant other, Ladonna. They have three dogs, and Charlize had a grand time running and playing with them. She's a sociable dog and gets along well with all the strangers we meet, human and canine.

I've known both Gary and Ladonna since 1956. Ladonna's late husband was also a classmate in veterinary school. Gary lost his wife to cancer a couple of years before our fiftieth class reunion. There was empathy for our shared experience, but we didn't dwell on it. We've visited together probably fewer than half a dozen times since our class graduated in 1960. Still, our conversation flowed easily.

Several of our veterinary school classmates were Korean War veterans, most of them married, some with children. Many of them lived in Veterans Village in Quonset huts and went to school on the GI Bill. Ladonna and her husband were among them. Sometimes the people, as represented by our government, do something right for everyone. In those days, not only the students were close; the wives, including Ladonna, were as well. They formed an auxiliary group making close friends. The wives shared experiences in difficult financial times but with a better future in the offing.

Many of those wives remained close, keeping in touch over the years. In my experience, the female of our species is much more efficient, determined, and relentless in the pursuit of friendship. That's how Gary and Ladonna found each other at our fiftieth year class reunion in Fort Collins, Colorado. Ladonna, widowed several years previously, attended the reunion to be with longtime female friends. Two lonely people with a shared history, both still grieving, met and made a connection. They now spend some of the year at her home in Nebraska and some of it at his home in Salinas, interspersed with travel for pleasure and enlightenment. They are comfortable together, not afraid to talk and reminisce about their prior lives with their well-loved spouses. I couldn't help but wonder if I would ever find someone and reach that place. Even better, their children and grandchildren are all happy that the two of them found each other. I wish them long and happy times together.

Thomas Wolfe and John Steinbeck were correct though. You can't go back and resume a past life, a former home, or even an old friendship. As our lives progress, we create new lives, new homes, new friendships. We might renew the friendships, but the relationships are different. The experiences of our past cannot be relived, except in memory. We and those old friends are different, made so by what life has sent our way and how we responded.

The three of us talked about our families and listened to each other politely but with wandering interest to the achievements of our offspring, whom we didn't really know. After we parted for the night, Charlize and I had an uninterrupted six hours of sleep in Frog. Gary, Ladonna, and I continued our conversation over breakfast in their home, but I was on a schedule, sort of. My son and his family in Carlsbad, California, had set aside time for Charlize and me in their hectic life, and we had to get down the road.

Goodbyes come easier for me now. Maybe they are not as important as they once were. Perhaps we'll spend time together again before our time is up, perhaps not. If we do find that our lives once more come together, we'll pick up comfortably, but I think we'll be careful to make our time together short enough so we retain the desire to meet and talk and catch up.

10

Frog Suffers a Wound

Before our stop in Salinas, I had neglected to refuel Old Blue, so by the time Charlize and I reached Monterey, the gas gauge was showing close to empty, and I was getting nervous. The first gas station I found was crowded. There were three rows of pumps, and the first two were full of vehicles refueling. The row closest to the inevitable convenience store selling overpriced indispensables was empty of vehicles, but a large truck delivering more of those indispensables was parked diagonally, blocking my ability to swing wide enough to line up with the gas pump.

I had made a sharp right turn into the station off a busy street, and Old Blue was past the first two rows of pumps. The pump islands were protected, actually guarded, by four-inch diameter steel posts planted firmly in the pavement and painted bright red. So I was both committed and stuck. Frog was still half in the street, blocking traffic in the near lane.

Inching forward, I thought I could maneuver far enough to my right and then back left to ease into the pump row. I checked both side-view mirrors. Yes, I thought, it's doable.

An impatient California driver, blocked by Frog, honked his horn. Rarely do I hear anyone honk in the environs of Seattle; it's just not considered good form.

Those red steel posts were closer and closer as I inched Old Blue forward and around them. Yes, I was going to clear them. Frog cleared the street, and traffic resumed. Now I was completely focused on the posts. Oops. There was a loud crunching noise. If I still had a stomach (but that's a whole other story), it would have turned inside out.

The cabin portion of Frog was exactly the same width as Old Blue. A major selling point for me was that she was built to travel over rough roads, made for camping, hunting, fishing—those kinds of activities. She had a significantly stronger frame than the average travel trailer, higher clearances, a heavy-duty axle, and oversized knobby tires. The wheels were outside the trailer cabin, so she actually was the width of both tires plus the truck. Aluminum fenders screwed onto the body of the cabin prevented mud, water, and snow or ice from splattering the cabin or any following vehicles. The fenders sported running lights fore and aft.

Anyway, while I was worrying about those painted red steel posts, I ignored the parked truck. The driver's side corner of the truck's rear bumper, also solid steel, made contact with the front running light of Frog's right side fender and scattered amber plastic over the pavement. With horns honking and people gathering to gawk, I got out to see how much damage I was responsible for. The front half of Frog's fender, now crumpled was separated from the cabin, and the screws were pulled loose. The bumper of the truck I hit sported a barely discernable scratch.

I managed to pull the fender off the tire and push the screws back into their ragged holes. Then, watching both sides carefully I was able, with much backing, forwarding, maneuvering, and wheel turning, to get around the corner and line up with the gas pump. Frog suffered her injury stoically, but there was no doubt she was struggling emotionally.

Duct tape is a wonder drug for all inanimate objects, a temporary fix but perhaps more versatile than baling wire. I used it to hold the fender in place and off the tire. Three days of travel later, the fender was still attached—sort of—but it was loosening. When I'd arrive in Carlsbad, California, I'd try to find someone to repair it properly and professionally. Maybe I'd try to fix it myself. My son has tools. Frog was too embarrassed to have a photo taken of the damage.

Throughout the ordeal, Charlize sensed my frustration and anger. She remained very quiet on her belly in Old Blue's back seat, chin resting on her paws, her eyes following me without judgment, without condemnation.

11

REDWOODS AND MORE

CHARLIZE AND I HAD BEEN ON THE ROAD for nine days when we stayed in an inexpensive but fancy RV park in Fortuna, California. The space rental was about the same as an economy motel. We had full service at our pull-through space, water, power, and TV cable, even a sewer hookup. The next day, we continued on US 101 until Leggett and then hooked up with Highway 1 hugging the coast. It was slow going but extremely scenic. We stopped at many vistas and a couple of tourist traps.

The weird-looking log half-buried in the sand caught my eye,
but Charlize wasn't interested.

I ate a late lunch in a tiny, quaint place featuring a *Wizard of Oz* theme. I savored my tasty salad loaded with Dungeness crab and had a nice conversation with the young waitress whose father was in the service in Iraq. She was worried about him, but I was at a complete loss to find any words that might reassure her. After lunch, we worked our way south, but the road was full of fifteen- to twenty-miles-per-hour curves, switchbacks, and steep grades.

During the day, we stopped at three different groves of redwood trees, only relatively small, protected remnants of what were once massive forests. Steinbeck ascribed almost god-like attributes to these three-thousand-plus-year-old behemoths. When Charlize and I were alone, walking amongst them, I did experience feelings similar to those I felt visiting old world synagogues whose congregants had been annihilated. Charlize was subdued, watching me closely mirroring the emotions I was feeling.

At three-thirty in the afternoon, we started looking for an RV park. The only ones seen we spotted after passing, and the road was too narrow to turn and go back. I stopped at a grocery store in Gualala, California, to purchase some fresh vegetables for dinner and was told where to find the California State Salt Point campground. At the gate to the campground, there was a friendly park ranger talking to a young couple that didn't stay. When I stopped, he told me to just pick a spot and then return and fill out an envelope at the gate, put five bucks in it, and I would be registered. I drove through the place and returned to the gate, too many choices.

When I stopped, he looked over and said, "You decide not to stay?"

"Nope, couldn't find an empty spot."

He looked at me incredulously until I smiled, and then he laughed politely at my lame joke. I climbed out of Old Blue to retrieve the envelope and made the loop again. I consulted with Charlize to pick a spot, filled out the envelope, and put in my five bucks.

*The deserted Salt Point Campground where
Charlize found something of interest.*

Here we were. There were no hookups for water, power, or cable, no Wi-Fi or cell phone connection, no sewer dump. The advantage was that, except for two senior ladies living in an RV as hosts of the campground, Charlize and I were the sole transient occupants. The ranger told us that if we walked down to the beach, about a half-mile jaunt, we might get a cell signal. Not worth the effort.

12

JERRY AND THE BIG SUR

W E LEFT MONTEREY, Frog nursing her broken fender. Before long, we were immersed in the beauty of the California Pacific Coast and Big Sur. It's difficult to keep the miles clicking along this coast with too many vistas calling out to be seen, experienced, and absorbed.

The amazing Big Sur.

About eleven o'clock in the morning, I decided it was time for a two-Splenda latte and before long found a roadside restaurant that advertised espresso. I pulled into a large parking area, separated from a front patio by a low rock wall. The same wide spot in the road housed a grocery store with the same architecture as the restaurant.

I instructed Charlize to guard Old Blue and went into the restaurant for my latte. During the short walk, I noticed a man sitting in the sun at one of a number of outdoor tables, avoiding the shade of the table's umbrella. He was eating what appeared to be a breakfast burrito. Our eyes met, he nodded, and I returned the nod.

When I came out, coffee in hand, our eyes met again. I walked toward him, and he motioned for me to sit down. He commented on Old Blue's Washington State license plates and Frog's unusual design. Before long, we were trading our life histories and thus passed a pleasant and illuminating half-hour, sitting in the warm sun with no place to be and nothing better to do. Sweet!

I excused myself and went to Old Blue to let Charlize out to do her business and to give her the opportunity to meet Jerry—that was his name—another graybeard like myself. Charlize didn't hesitate. She walked directly to Jerry and made friends. Most dogs are good judges of character, and I trust Charlize's judgment in that regard. While we talked, Charlize found some shade under the table and took a snooze, content to be close.

I learned that Jerry lived in his truck, moving from one campground to another as the time limit for occupancy expired. It was a routine broken only by an occasional trip to Monterey to visit his daughter and to pick up his Social Security check. He's an artist—one of too many to count with talent but no luck and no sponsor. Actually, he never said he was an artist, only that he drew pictures, but the life history I extracted from him included an unfinished engineering degree and time spent as a draftsman until computer assisted drafting (CAD) made that profession obsolete. Even though that was followed by various positions in the corporate world, nothing seemed to hold his interest very long. He became a set designer and painter and described a litany of jobs and experiences, including more than one wife, several girlfriends, and at least the one daughter he mentioned.

Jerry was a little deficient in hygiene. I was careful to stay upwind. Most would probably classify him as a bum, at the least homeless, which technically he was, discounting the truck that I never saw. But he was easy to talk to and a terrific listener who quickly found out why I was on the road, how I came to be at that place at that time, and what Charlize's role was in our odyssey. His story was as interesting to me as, to all appearances, mine was to him We were two strangers who sat comfortably in the sun and talked of life and philosophy and politics, both corporate and academic. We solved no problems, came to no decisions, found no solutions, nor even consensus about those problems that we discussed. We parted as friends, only knowing first names, probably never to meet again but both of us satisfied with the hour and a half we had spent together in gainful conversation. At least Charlize and I were.

13

CHARLIZE THE BULLY

NEVER WOULD I HAVE ANTICIPATED IT. Of all the dogs I've been responsible for, Charlize is the friendliest and the calmest dog around strangers. When we arrived at my son's home in Carlsbad, she met their golden retriever, Bentley, for the first time. I've known Bentley since they got him as a puppy when they still lived in Vancouver, British Columbia, before moving to Southern California. Bentley is a lovable lug, typical of the breed, a vacuum cleaner when it comes to food, with a happy-go-lucky, what-me-worry outlook on life. He outweighs Charlize by at least twenty pounds, maybe more.

When we first arrived, the two of them dashed madly around the house, narrowly avoiding breaking anything. My son turned them loose in their exquisitely planned and immaculately executed backyard that mimics the garden of a Mediterranean villa. The two dogs rushed about, banging into each other, tearing up the lawn with their toenails, and having a grand time.

It wasn't long before Charlize noticed one of Bentley's toys, grabbed it, ran off to the corner of the yard, and lay down with the toy between her front legs. Bentley stood stock-still, not understanding, making no effort to retrieve his toy.

Are you just going to leave both of us out here?

After a while, the whole family, including the dogs, went indoors. Now Charlize had access to a cornucopia of toys and took advantage of the opportunity. She gathered several of Bentley's chew toys and deposited them on a carefully chosen spot on the floor. Bentley went over to retrieve one of them, and Charlize rushed over, growling, and chased him away. After Charlize had deposited all the toys she could find on her chosen spot, she again lay down with the toys between her front legs and dared Bentley to try to take any of them. He didn't respond to the tease, just stood, cocking his head from side to side, trying his best to understand.

Do you want this ball?

It was time to feed the dogs. To avoid confrontation, Bentley was given his food in his regular place inside while I fed Charlize outside on the patio. As I said, Bentley scarfs up his food like a vacuum cleaner whereas Charlize is lady-like. She eats slowly, carefully chewing each mouthful, and frequently does a little walkabout and then returns for another mouthful or two. She rarely eats everything in her dish, leaving a few kibbles. Her mother must have taught her that proper manners dictate leaving a little food on your plate. As usual, she left some food in her dish and asked to come inside, so I let Bentley out to clean up the leftovers. He got within two feet of her dish, his intent obvious, and Charlize rushed out, shouldered him aside with a low growl, and swiftly dispatched the remaining kibbles. So my mild-mannered companion does harbor a mean streak after all.

14

ANOTHER SIDE OF
CHARLIZE'S PERSONALITY

WE LEFT FROG IN CARLSBAD and headed for Phoenix to spend time with my brother and his family and look up some old friends from my early days practicing veterinary medicine. We're of an age when, unfortunately, many of my veterinary friends are no longer with us, so it becomes more and more important to visit those who are still here. After the sojourn in Phoenix, I planned to return to my son's home, pick up Frog, and head back north.

My friends Don and Susie were visiting their daughter, who lives in Scottsdale, a Phoenix suburb. Don and I were roommates for three years at Colorado State University when it was still Colorado A & M. He's been my closest friend since 1954, even though he ranches in the Sandhills of Nebraska, and we're able to get together only occasionally. We were lucky that Rosalie and Susie became fast friends, as it's rare for all four in two couples to be close and enjoy each other's company. Whenever we were able to get together, the conversation seemed to pick up where last we left it, as though we had been together the previous day.

After averaging between eight and eleven miles per gallon and straining to reach fifty-five miles per hour pulling Frog, Old Blue, freed of that load, averaged sixteen and a half miles per gallon while traveling seventy-five miles an hour on the freeways between San

Diego and Phoenix. With gasoline costing $4.20 or more per gallon in the San Diego area, I calculated that I saved at least fifty-two dollars on the trip to Phoenix, and I anticipated saving an equal amount on my return.

My brother and his wife provided free room and board during my stay. I could have become used to that! They are owned by a Chihuahua mix, short on stature and gigantic on attitude, like many of her ilk. She's also possessive. When we walked in their front door, that little dog—her name is Madeline—let Charlize know whose house it was and that trespassers would be barely tolerated, at best. Charlize learned quickly to avoid her as much as possible. Madeline seized any opportunity to attack, nipping at Charlize's hind legs, going for the Achilles tendon. Charlize cowered and ran away, but I feared that at some point, probably when none of us was witnesses, she would turn on Madeline and do serious harm.

Madeline keeping her distance for the time being.

My brother, Joe, and his wife, Carol, own an acre lot filled with well-kept desert vegetation. The landscaping is unique, neat, and starkly beautiful—if you grew up here in the desert and like it. I did and I do.

While retrieving for my two grandnieces, Charlize ran into a cactus. She now understands to avoid those denizens of the desert (the cacti, not the nieces).

My nephew, Andy, his wife, Ingrid, and the girls, Naomi and her older sister, Mathilda, live in Germany. Andy and the two girls were visiting, but Ingrid was busy with her class at the University of Erlanger and had remained at home.

At four o'clock in the morning, my first night here, Naomi, almost four years old, got out of her bed and came into the room where her daddy had been sleeping prior to Charlize's and my arrival. Daddy, my nephew Andy, was asleep on a blow-up mattress in the same room with his two daughters.

Little Naomi walked over the mattress where her dad slumbered, came into the room where Charlize and I were ensconced behind a closed door, and got into the bed where I was asleep on my right side. She was at my back, so she crawled over me to get to my front side and announced that she wanted to snuggle. Charlize, ever watchful, helped Naomi up onto the bed, nuzzling her behind.

I guess I didn't feel or snuggle the same as Daddy, so Naomi started to fidget.

"I'm your Uncle Dave," I said drowsily. "Do you want your daddy to snuggle with you?"

"Yes!" she answered.

"He's in your room sleeping on a mattress on the floor. Do you want to go there to be with him?"

"Yes," she replied and left, apparently nonplussed by the situation.

Both Naomi and Mathilda are completely bilingual. Andy usually speaks to them in English, and they speak to him in English. Their mother, a native German, speaks to them in German, and they speak to her in kind. If they are in a situation where everyone is speaking German, Andy also speaks German. Their mother does the same in English when she's in an English-speaking situation. Andy tells me that when he first spoke German to the girls or their mother spoke

English, they were confused and a little upset that the parent was not communicating with them properly. As they grew older, they adjusted well, so now, no matter which language is being used in the conversation, they answer in kind. Oh, to be so facile with language!

15

Changes in People and Places

The longer I live, the more apparent it is to me that my friends and family change—not their basic personalities but their attitudes, their belief systems. I note this especially because as they get older, their lives and mine lack a continuum of shared experience. We may be wiser about some things—maybe not. These changes in yourself and in the people you once knew well make it difficult to go back, to go home. Perhaps more difficult, at least in this country of untrammeled growth, are the changes to the place that was always home.

I guess I'll always think of Phoenix as home. Both Rosalie and I grew up there. We went to grade school and high school there. At the time, Phoenix had only three high schools: Phoenix Union, North, and West. I went to North. Rosalie, a year behind me, went to West. It's probably a good thing we didn't know each other then. When I graduated from North High in 1954, I suppose no more than a hundred thousand people were living in Phoenix.

In 1961, after graduating from veterinary school, I opened the Paradise Animal Hospital in Paradise Valley, on the corner of Thirty-second Street and Bell Road. The closest subdivision was a mile or two south, toward Phoenix. There might have been a hundred homes scattered in the desert in the ten or so miles between the hospital and Cave Creek. The town of Carefree was just beginning to build.

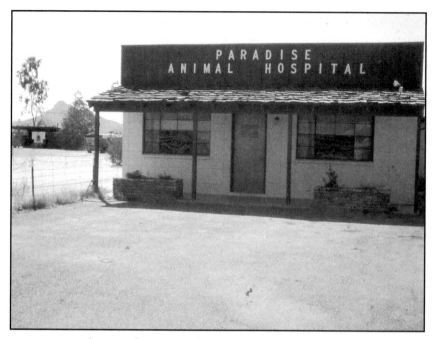

The Paradise Animal Hospital, summer of 1961.

Rosalie and I left Phoenix with our sons in 1970 when I went back to school to earn a PhD from Ohio State University. There was one freeway, the Black Canyon Highway. I can't count or keep track of the number of freeways in and around Phoenix now—too many. My old veterinary clinic is now a store that sells imported Mexican furniture, pots, and decorator items. That corner is close to the middle of the greater Phoenix area's population. The formerly empty desert is now full of strip malls and homes, all the way to Cave Creek.

Not long ago, my brother and his wife moved to a new, for them, home just south of Cave Creek. Nothing is the same. The Valley of the Sun has too many people, too many new buildings, and way too much congestion. Many of the places I remember fondly are gone, and I'm uncomfortable with the changes. Progress? I'm not so certain.

All these changes force me to dwell on how things were, how they used to be. In the desert summer, one hundred-plus degrees, before air-conditioning, the temperature dropped ten or more degrees when the water truck went through our old neighborhood, dampening the dirt road to hold down the dust before all the dads came home from work. When it was time for us kids to go to bed, Mom gave us wet sheets, and we rolled up in them on cots in the back yard. The stars and moon were so bright that we could read by them. Dad would carry the three of us, sound asleep, into the house before he went to bed.

Just after World War II ended, my dad brought home a swamp cooler and installed it in a living room window. The neighbors would come over in the evening to sit in front of it and enjoy the blast of air cooled by water dripping down through excelsior pads. In the early 1950s, the same phenomena occurred when Dad brought home a TV with the little round screen. I'm sounding like an old man!

Charlize, happy in my brother's backyard near Cave Creek, Arizona.

16

FIRST TRIP TO SAN DIEGO

DURING THE DRIVE from San Diego to Phoenix, I remembered the first time I made that journey—but from the other direction, Phoenix to San Diego. I was ten years old in the summer of 1946. World War II was over, and my Uncle Sol, my dad's younger brother, was being mustered out of the Seabees. We made the trip in our 1940 Chevy before the multi-fabric and multi-color upholstery and the loss of running boards and fenders. The Chevy had new tires but no air-conditioning. In fact, I don't remember a heater in that car—at least not a functioning one.

To beat the summer heat, we started after dark, and Dad drove all night. No freeways or interstate highways to travel at seventy-five miles an hour. I don't think Dad ever got that car over fifty. No radio either, not that there would have been a radio station to connect to anywhere in that desert—well, maybe in Yuma.

My brother and sister and I were supposed to be sleeping in the back seat, but I remember waking up and eavesdropping on the quiet conversation between Mom and Dad. They were talking to stay awake, and the conversation was mundane, everyday subjects and their hopes and dreams, mostly concerning us kids.

Sonoran Desert in February, a beautiful, restful place.

The road frequently dipped down and then up, through many gullies and washes, no bridges. I was concerned because there were many stories about entire families being washed away in their car by a flash flood. Those natural disasters originated when it rained in the mountains, sending a wall of water gushing through those desert washes with no warning.

Old Blue, Charlize, and I made that trip from Phoenix to San Diego during daylight hours on the interstate at seventy-five miles an hour. The radio was tuned to a station playing jazz, and we had air-conditioning. The trip was different, but better? Maybe. What was the rush?

17

PREPARING FOR LEG TWO
OF THE ODYSSEY

AFTER OUR TWELVE-DAY HIATUS in Phoenix, Charlize and I made it back to Carlsbad where we found that Frog's refrigerator was no longer functioning. For reasons unknown, when I changed LP gas tanks, the refrigerator continued to run on the battery or direct electrical hook-up but not on gas. So I took her to a guy who repairs appliances on RVs.

Carlsbad has many, many RV parks and experienced people to service them. Turns out it was just a loose wire to the igniter. I had thought that the igniter might be the problem, but I had no idea where it was, how to get to it, or how to fix it if I found it. But the service guy fixed it, and all systems were functional.

The next Sunday morning, my son Jeff and I took Bentley and Charlize to the Delmar Dog Beach at Delmar, California, south of Carlsbad. Charlize seemed to forget about stealing Bentley's toys, and they were good buddies again.

Charlize surprised me again by going into the water enthusiastically—an uncommon behavior for a German shepherd. Several dogs were in the area, well behaved for the most part, particularly our two. When I used the throwing stick to get her ball well out into the surf, Charlize was completely focused on retrieving that ball. While engaged in this very serious game, she ignored all the other dogs, including

Bentley, and brought the ball back for me to throw it again and again as far out as I could chuck it.

Dog park people are an interesting group. Whenever either Charlize or Bentley interacted with another dog, Jeff and I inevitably engaged in a conversation with the owner.

Charlize in hot pursuit of her tennis ball.

"How old are your dogs? They seem to get along so well," one of them inquired.

"We're not sure about Charlize. She was adopted from a shelter, and we don't have any history on her. I'd say about three or four years old. Bentley is four."

"Are you from around here? I thought I saw you get out of a truck with Washington plates."

"I live in Edmonds, just north of Seattle. We're here visiting with my son and his family—and his dog."

It wasn't difficult to extract their life history without revealing my own. The dog people of Southern Californian seem to be a garrulous lot, more interested in telling their life stories than hearing those of others. I refrained from providing anything of real interest, and Jeff volunteered nothing.

18

CONTEMPLATING THE SEA, NATURE, AND PHILOSOPHY

THE NEXT MORNING, Charlize and I were on the road again, following the coast. The plan was to head north, wandering. We made it a short day, and after setting up Frog, Charlize and I took a walk and sat on the beach. I took a pocket edition of John Steinbeck's *Grapes of Wrath* out and read aloud to Charlize. She sat directly in front of me, her head cocked to one side, ears erect, listening intently. After a thirty- or forty-year hiatus, I was returning to my favorite author.

I read differently these days—not surprising with so many additional years to experience life and interpret and perhaps even understand what I'm reading. Steinbeck points out the good human qualities of wisdom, tolerance, kindliness, generosity, and humility. Good humans live moral, ethical lives, practice the Golden Rule, deal honestly and transparently with others, and don't cut corners or press to see how much wealth, power, or prestige they can accumulate without having to answer for their methods.

Bad people demonstrate cruelty, greed, self-interest, graspingness, and rapacity. They do their best to take advantage of others and believe their worth is determined by how much wealth, power, and prestige they accumulate. They are sharp dealers who take advantage of every opportunity to attain more and ignore or avoid ethical and even legal issues whenever they believe they can get away with it. They push the boundaries of acceptable behavior.

A seascape promoting the contemplation of life.

Steinbeck reckoned that our American society almost always judges the second group to be successful while the first group—those millions lacking wealth, power, or prestige—are considered unsuccessful. I fervently hope this jaded view isn't true, although our society does seem to idolize individuals who accumulate things, through whatever means, and considers them to be successful.

The rub is that these accumulators, especially as they age, often become philanthropists and rediscover morality and ethics. Sometimes they even rediscover the great teacher of those values—religion. Think of Carnegie, Rockefeller, Astor, and the various railroad and mining robber barons. The list could include many more recent examples that garnered inordinate wealth and power from new technologies or financial shenanigans. Society overlooks their lack of morality and ethical behavior while acquiring massive wealth because they were, or are, judged to be successful and managed, for the most part, to avoid prosecution. We anoint these individuals as smart business people and give them respect, if not adoration.

The probable truth is that all of us have some characteristics of both groups. The division is not so stark, not so black and white. Perhaps our society does accommodate shades of gray behavior that allow an individual to make minor trespasses but, for the most part, live a moral, ethical life and still be considered successful. But then, I believed in the tooth fairy for a long time.

19

THE MOHAVE DESERT

FOLLOWING MY NOSE and my desire to wander along new highways, I decided to turn south and east. For two days, Charlize and I drove through the Mohave Desert. It's different, very different from the Sonoran Desert, full of a variety of interesting cacti, including the majestic saguaro, where I grew up hiking and camping, dealing with the heat before universal air conditioning. As a kid, I loved the harsh environment that required skill and knowledge to survive.

From Indio to Lake Havasu and from there to the Zion National Park, we drove through the Mohave. In my book, *Man Hunt*, I wrote about a trip that Tom Tobin took from the Taos area to Los Angeles in the 1850s. As was always the case in those days, the trip through the Mohave, from one watering place to the next, was brutal, the route marked by the skeletons of man and beast.

Charlize's and my trip was a piece of cake. Old Blue, with Frog closely following, clicked off the miles of pavement at a steady pace. The uninitiated might consider the Mohave dull, repetitious, mile after mile of sand, rocks, sagebrush, and monotony. But it isn't. The flora constantly changed before our eyes as we moved north and east. It was still too early for the desert to burst into full bloom, but no fewer than two hundred different wild flowers and cacti were celebrating life in that so-called wasteland. I spotted early Mojave gold poppy along the roadside, their bright yellow flowers waving to us on narrow leafless stems, oscillating in the slipstream as we blew past at sixty miles per hour.

The most common plant I saw was the creosote bush. I know it as greasewood, an evergreen that can grow upwards of four feet. When we stopped to stretch our legs and for Charlize to water the desert, I spotted green ephedra, also known as Mormon tea. In the southern part of our journey that day, the land was full of sagebrush, salt brush, and greasewood.

As we traveled north, we passed through various, fairly well-defined eco-zones, dominated by several varieties of yucca, including tall yucca that were almost tree-like, just beginning to form blossoms. I also saw chaparral and, in the washes, palo verde and mesquite.

Mohave Desert from Old Blue at sixty miles per hour.

We followed California State Route 74 diagonally across the desert to Indio, passing through the Santa Rosa and San Jacinto Mountain Ranges. Above 3,500 feet, I saw some California juniper. In lower areas, where there was water, tamarisk trees and palms flourished. When I was growing up, we had a small grove of tamarisk on one corner of our lot. They were at least forty feet tall, with dark purplish bark. The leaves don't look like normal leaves; they're more like scales, salt-encrusted, dirty. We used to climb those trees but always needed a bath afterward. You don't see those dirty, trashy trees much anymore. They've been replaced by more modern landscaping.

The Mojave Desert is somehow more forbidding, starker, more desolate than my familiar Sonoran Desert. The Sonoran Desert is full of many varieties of cacti. It must have been a fairly wet fall and winter in the areas of the Mohave that we drove through because I saw a lot of grass.

We worked our way up through an area of pinion pines that gave way to another agave and yucca eco-zone. Arriving at the Cahuilla Tewanet Overlook, we exited Old Blue to take in what seemed like hundreds of miles of visibility. This desert mountain area is home to the endangered peninsular bighorn sheep, but although I instructed Charlize to keep a sharp eye on the lookout for them, they managed to escape our attention. I did spot a golden eagle soaring in the azure sky, taking advantage of the updrafts. I pointed out the bird to Charlize, but she didn't seem to be able to focus on it.

Charlize sitting next to the national monument plaque.

Charlize found a comfortable spot to rest next to the national monument plaque which read:

In this place of Solitude and Beauty,
Please take time to show respect
For both the natural surroundings
And those who share this highway.

Maintain a grateful awareness of the
Time given you
To share with your Loved Ones
And remember those who innocently lost
What you may take for granted.

Please Drive Safely

Santa Rosa and San Jacinto Mountains National Monument

I wiped tears from my eyes, still trying to deal with Rosalie's death.

20

Zion, Bryce, and Awesome Back Roads

Growing up in Arizona, I spent significant time camping and hiking in both the Grand Canyon and Oak Creek Canyon, along with a whole summer working on the Navajo Reservation. These experiences produced a serious flaw in me: I'm less than overcome by emotion when viewing wind-and-water sculpted red rock formations.

Charlize and I spent a comfortable night in Frog in an RV park in Springdale, Utah. Early the next morning, we did a quick tour of Zion National Park. It's beautiful, but as I said …

We followed the Zion-Mount Carmel Highway through a mile-long tunnel carved out of the rock and stopped at an overview just outside of the east entrance. There I talked with three very friendly young folks: Jim, who is about to graduate from nursing school and two female nursing students from the same school in St. George, Utah.

Charlize initiated contact and obviously enjoyed the attention and petting that the young ladies provided. The conversation flowed easily. All three were bright, interested, committed, and determined to do good and make a difference. Jim wanted to be involved in a medical program that helps underserved patients in a Third World country. It's uplifting to find young folks who are committed to service and to making the world a better place. I hope society will judge these three as successful!

Charlize checking out the view.

Charlize and I arrived at Bryce Canyon about noon and did a quick tour. We weren't allowed to take Frog beyond the first viewpoint, Sunrise Point. To tour the rest of the park, we would have had to unhitch and leave Frog unattended. Charlize wasn't happy with that idea, and neither was I, so we departed.

Rather than backtrack, we made a command decision and headed east on State Highway 12. We stopped in Tropic, Utah, for a quick lunch—just your normal hamburger and French fries, nothing special—and then we pressed on. The road carried only an occasional vehicle, and we didn't see a single eighteen-wheeler.

We stopped for a panoramic view at the mountain pass between Escalante and Boulder. The plaque stated that the CCC had constructed "Million Dollar Road" with "skill, sweat and dynamite," finishing it in 1940. The view spanned from Navajo Mountain on the Utah-Arizona border to the east, the Henry Mountains in the middle, and west to the Aquarius Plateau and Boulder Mountain. The distance from east to west must be well over a hundred miles. The vista includes a cornucopia of deep, winding canyons that form the Escalante River Basin.

Charlize enjoying the snow at the top of one of the passes.

After leaving Bryce, we traversed at least three summit passes. The highest was about 9,600 feet, and there was snow on the ground. We arrived at the beautiful Fruita Campground in Capitol Reef National Park about four thirty in the afternoon. With my Senior National Parks and Federal Recreational Lands Pass, it cost only five bucks for the night. I was tired from all the mountain driving but pleased with the full day. It was an awesome reliving of the past to drive on mostly empty, two-lane highways—reminiscent of the way driving in the West used to be when I was young.

21

THE FRUITA CAMPGROUND

W E DROVE THROUGH THE ENVIRONS of the Fruita Campground, another red rock canyon. This one is the product of wind and the Fremont River, flowing gently in early March but still the color of the sand and silt it is transporting to help clog Lake Powell.

The campground is on the site of some old homesteads, and it features several fruit and nut orchards. I identified apricot trees for certain but was unable to determine the other kinds of fruit and couldn't tell from the bare trees.

During our evening and morning walks, Charlize and I saw many deer and three unconcerned, wild turkeys that Charlize wanted desperately to catch. Fat chance. The fruit trees are protected from the deer—and elk, which are in the vicinity as well—by two lines of defense, one wire cage inside a larger one. The trees were well cared for, I presume by Bureau of Land Management personnel (although I don't know that for certain). We were visiting too early in the season for the well-publicized explosion of flowering trees, but by all accounts it is a spectacular display.

The Fremont River gently waters the microclimate of this picturesque canyon—which is more than just another red rock canyon. The palette includes a plethora of yellows, oranges, and purples in moving shadows and blazes of sunlight. This place attracted Mormon settlers in the 1880s. I'm tempted to return to find out where these people came from, how they acquired the fruit trees they planted, and what their lives were like. This will be one more addition to my expanding, rather than shrinking, bucket list.

While taking Charlize for her evening constitutional, we met an interesting young couple. Charlize, as usual, initiated the contact. They both work as counselors at a type of boot camp for juvenile offenders, and most of their young charges have drug problems. They told me they currently are working with sixty-seven of these youngsters, teaching them wilderness survival skills, as well as how to cope with today's real-world problems.

They were preparing their dinner—burritos wrapped in aluminum foil, heating on a grate over a too-large wood fire. The young lady kept moving the three burritos around, presumably to keep them from burning. They invited us to share their meal, but Charlize and I had already had dinner.

Charlize waiting for her breakfast at the Fruita Campground.

22

THE FUTURE OF THE
COLORADO RIVER DAMS

Our journey from the Fruita Campground to the San Luis Valley took us over the upper reaches of Lake Powell, straddling the border between Arizona and Utah. I assume the engineers and planners who proposed, designed, and built the Glen Canyon Dam on the Colorado River anticipated the amount of water-borne debris that would end up in the lake. After setting up Frog for the night in Blanca, Colorado, I checked Google (the source of all information, right or wrong) for the dam to find out how much silt and sediment goes into the lake and what the long-term effects will be. Somewhere between 65,000 and 100,000 cubic yards of sediment reach the lake per year. A study conducted in the mid-1970s used sonar to measure the sediment. That study concluded that the lake could hold about seven hundred years of accumulated sediment.

Not surprisingly, I found many articles forecasting doom and destruction while vilifying the engineers and planners who promoted the Glen Canyon Dam project. All the arguments seemed well made and were supported by presumably scientific studies. I found an almost equal number of well-written articles touting the economic, recreational, agricultural, and social benefits of the dams on the Colorado River. These articles also cited scientific evidence claiming that, although the dams could eventually fail without mitigation, there is no imminent danger. These proponents of the dams argue that there are ways to flush the lake using the jet tubes and spillways of the dam.

I don't have any idea how much accumulation there is at the dam, but at Hick's Crossing, with the level of the lake down considerably, the amount of silt and sediment deposited in the upper reaches of the high-water marks was evident, and I could see places where that stuff was falling into the water. After reading those articles, I feel strongly ... both ways.

Charlize checking out the lowered water levels of Lake Powell.

The controversy about the Colorado River dams and their long-term effects on the environment and water use rages on. What seems apparent is that predictions and study results are equivocal: Nobody knows for certain what will happen. If political action or the inevitable progression of nature takes away the Glen Canyon and the downstream dams, many predict a domino effect in which the mega concentrations of people in Southern California and Arizona, along with the agricultural and recreational enterprises of that area, will be desperate to find water.

The question seems to be more when than if. Opponents say it could happen two generations from now and could be sudden and catastrophic. Proponents say nothing will happen for many life-times—maybe as long as seven hundred years. I have no idea what to believe, but the longer I live, the more I feel that way about most arguments … ambivalent.

Charlize seemed puzzled about my concerns over the greatly reduced water levels of these upper reaches of Lake Powell. I tried to point out the large accumulations of sediment, now high and dry as the drought continues. I thought I might get a photo of her looking at them with some level of concern in her expression. No such luck.

23
HUNTING FOR MAN HUNT

CHARLIZE AND I SPENT TWO DAYS in the San Luis Valley trying to visit the places I'd identified while researching my historical novel, *Man Hunt*. The book is a fictionalized account of the intersecting lives of real people—Tom Tobin, a frontiersman, and the Espinosas, a family of New Mexicans. After the Mexican-American War, the entire village in which the Espinosas lived lost their communal property and became destitute. The Espinosa brothers responded by turning to robbery, murder, and a bloody vendetta against the gringos.

Many of the places mentioned in my book were identified and described in historical accounts and records made during the lives of these people. Several years ago, Rosalie and I visited Taos, New Mexico, and passed through some of the places I wrote about in the book, but at that time, I had no idea that I would be writing about those venues in the future.

A reconstructed Fort Garland sits on the original site of that fort. Some portions of the original buildings remain, along with historical records of what the fort actually looked like when it was an active army post. It was the same as I pictured it from my reading and study of existing drawings. The museum at the fort provides insight into the lives of the soldiers who were stationed in that wilderness outpost, as well as reconstructions of their sleeping quarters and artifacts of daily life, such as cooking and eating utensils and uniforms. The site is an interesting place for children and adults to gain some understanding of that time and place.

Charlize and I traveled from Fort Garland south to Taos. Along the way, I tried to identify the location of Tobin's Trinchera Ranch, but other than the general area where it should have been, I couldn't find the specific site. We passed through the town of Cochilla, near where Tobin had a farm and kept his family. Nobody I asked knew where his farm had been located, nor did they recognize the name. Discouraging.

We visited the museums at the homes of Governor Bent and Kit Carson, and they were as I remembered them from our previous visit, smaller than today's expectations of the homes of famous people. Walking through Governor Bent's home and seeing the rooms where his family hid and he eventually died in the Taos Revolt made those events come alive for me. Unfortunately, Charlize was not allowed to see these places, but I told her all about them when I returned and let her out of Old Blue to water the dusty parking lot we had parked in.

After getting Old Blue serviced in Taos, Charlize and I drove around on several back roads in the Arroyo Hondo area. We even stopped to ask some local folks if they could direct me to the site of Turley's mill, a prominent historical landmark mentioned in my reference books. I couldn't find it, and those I asked couldn't or wouldn't help. Maybe they just didn't want another nosy tourist poking around in their neighborhood.

The next day, we continued our hunt to identify some of the sites where the Espinosas did their deadly deeds, but without much luck. Time and the new positioning of roads and highways have changed the landscape.

Late in the afternoon, we gave up and made a side trip to the Great Sand Dunes National Park. This place was interesting and informative. The natural forces of water flow, wind, the location in front of a mountain range with the necessary configuration to direct the prevailing winds, and the geological rift effect all combine to create and maintain a reasonably large area of pure sand dunes.

Charlize looking for the ocean that should be associated with this large beach.

The size and shape of the dunes are in a state of constant change. The largest dune is more than seven hundred feet above the valley floor. Charlize finally decided that the place was nothing more than a huge sandbox for her to frolic in.

The next day, we drove over La Veta Pass, and again I was unable to locate the landmarks described in my research on the nefarious activities of the Espinosas. An explanation came on the eastern side of the pass when I spotted a sign identifying the old La Veta Pass road. It took a different direction from the paved highway we were on and probably different from the wagon trail when Tobin was active in the area.

The changes in landscape, experience, and lifestyle of the people now living in the various environments we pass through are a recurring theme of this odyssey. I tend to focus on changes over my lifetime, but piled onto the historical changes I formerly read about. Thinking about places and the events in those places in the past is a comfortable exercise. I don't have to deal with things as they are now. Is this just one more sign of my age?

24

CLASSMATES

WHILE DRIVING IN SAN DIEGO, and now in Denver, I can hear my own voice complaining, speaking aloud, but it is as if I am out-of-body, away but close enough to hear myself ranting. I'm just another old geezer, complaining that everything has changed and not for the better. All this growth isn't progress ... or is it?

I have a good friend in Denver, actually in the suburb of Littleton. His name is also Charley, but without the weird spelling. I've known him since 1954. We were on the swimming team together at what was then Colorado A & M and became Colorado State University while we were still in attendance. On road trips, we were roommates. We also both got into veterinary school the same year, so we're classmates as well. As I said, *good* friends, but how did we ever get this old? He agreed that he still thinks the same way he did when he was in his thirties or forties, as do I.

After Charlize and I arrived in Denver, we spent the next three days and nights with Charley and his wonderful wife, Jean. It was therapeutic.

My friend Charley is a natural politician. He remembers people's names—of those he meets, of their spouses, of their kids. And he actually cares when he asks how they're all doing. During my stay, everywhere we went, he ran into people he knew, and he always took the time to greet them and ask about them and their families by name. In every restaurant we entered, the cute young servers and hosts or hostesses knew Charley by sight and came over to hug and greet him, and he immediately connected with each of them. I know he works hard at it, but the true gift is that he cares enough to do it.

Charley's grandfather was the kingmaker in Colorado politics in the 1930s and 1940s, maybe longer. I guess that's where my friend comes by this talent.

Charlize exploring Cheeseman Park near the Denver Botanical Gardens.

We stayed in Denver just three days. On the day we left, I woke up early so we would be well ahead of a predicted snowstorm. We were on the road by 4:30 a.m. After the three-day hiatus, it was comfortable driving, so we pressed on all day and into the evening, avoiding the storm by driving north and west.

About eight o'clock in the evening, we arrived at the home of another classmate, Lionel, who lives in Nampa, Idaho. After a long, satisfying day, Charlize and I were warmly welcomed. We spent the evening and more than half of the next day visiting and catching up. Lionel and his wife had been at our veterinary class reunion the previous October, so they were surprised and saddened to hear of Rosalie's passing. Rosalie had put up a brave front when we all had last been together.

Charley and Lionel both built hugely successful equine veterinary practices that have now been taken over by veterinarians they originally hired as associates then taken as partners. Both of these practices provide specialized veterinary care for their own clients and for many referred to them by other veterinarians.

I'm so proud of all of my classmates. They've made significant contributions to society and to the profession. At least six of us ended up in academia, teaching the next generations of veterinarians. Charley was president of the AAEP, the American Association of Equine Practitioners, and another classmate was president of the AVMA, the American Veterinary Medicine Association. Many served at presidents of their local AVMA chapters and went on to more responsible positions at the regional level. All those who went into practice were successful and provided professional and state-of-the-art veterinary care for their patients and their clients. Many lives have been well spent, and we're all still looking forward.

When I questioned my classmates at our least reunion about how they are dealing with being on the wrong side of seventy-five, they all agreed with me. None of us thought that we feel or think differently than we did just out of school. But we all have aches and pains to complain about, and most of us are gimping around. The true revelation comes when we look in the mirror!

25

HOME

CHARLIZE DIDN'T REALIZE WE WERE HOME. While we were traveling, at six thirty or so each morning, she'd press her cold nose on my cheek and utter a soft whine to get me up. I'd let her out of Frog or the house of the people we were staying with, usually on her extendable leash. After she'd done her business, we'd get on with whatever the day had in store. We had places to go, things to see, people to meet. Now, I wanted to sleep in. Fat chance.

We'd wandered for well over a month, and every day, it seemed, I was asking questions of myself about Rosalie's death and what my life would be. There were no answers. I suppose the discovery that it was possible to make decisions unilaterally after almost fifty-three years of collaborating (or at least consulting) came to me so gradually that I didn't notice. Of course, I discuss everything with Charlize, but she has yet to voice a comprehensible opinion, except for exuberant enthusiasm for walks and playing ball.

Now at home, I've gone through thirty-nine days of accumulated mail, paid the overdue bills I hadn't been able to identify online, and restocked the refrigerator. Now what? During our travels, I rekindled some old friendships, and now I have to work at keeping them viable and active. That will require both time and effort.

Frog needs some repairs and renovations to improve her ability to travel rough roads. I was disappointed with how she responded to the rough spots we hit along the way. They are just minor things, though. She needs better access to the storage space under the bed and clasps on cupboard doors and drawers to prevent them from coming open when I hit a bump in the road. And she needs a method of keeping the table from sliding and banging around loose and into the corner of the cupboard and the refrigerator. I should be able to get her in good shape for our next adventure, planned for May.

My writing projects have kept me busy. I recently completed a crime novel, as yet unnamed. I finally finished another round of editing it, done, I hope, for a while. Now I have to start submitting it to agents and publishers.

I also started researching a new project that I'm excited about: Samuel Ha-Nagid was born near the end of the tenth century. He was a rabbi who wrote poetry dealing with love and God and wine and war in Hebrew and Arabic. Some of his poetry survives today. He also became the indispensable right hand of the caliph of Granada, his vizier, and eventually the commanding general of the caliph's armies. Ha Nagid was never defeated on the field of battle.

They were a team—a Muslim ruler and a Jewish advisor and commander in a time of enlightenment, education, literacy, and tolerance that lasted for more than three hundred years during the so-called Dark Ages. There's a story to be told, but it will necessitate a trip to Granada, Spain, for research.

26

Dogs and Porcupines

SCREAMING AT A TODDLER not to touch something hot can be effective sometimes, but not nearly as effective, long-term, as allowing that curious mind to experience pain. The same is true of dogs, although they seem to have slightly more built-in survivorship skills than toddlers do, with one exception I can think of: porcupines. As a vet, I can't tell you how many times I've pulled porcupine quills from the muzzle, nose, and face of the same dogs. They never seem to learn.

Maybe it's the chase. Rabbits, squirrels, all those creatures that run and rarely get caught are a source of pleasure. Dogs love the thrill of the chase. But porcupines are disdainful. They scurry, but not quite fast enough to avoid the catch. Maybe they enjoy the inevitable result, knowing they will prevail.

Roger was a boxer dog that never learned. The first time I saw him, his head was as big as a soccer ball, filled with porcupine quills and swollen with inflammation. After anesthetizing the poor guy, I spent almost two hours laboriously pulling quills out of him, one at a time. I saw him at least three more times, not nearly as loaded with quills but obviously not hurt enough to learn, or maybe he had attention deficit disorder. And he wasn't the only dog I encountered with a similar problem when it came to porcupines.

Charlize, unhappy in a "sit-stay" in front of cholla cacti.

The same phenomenon doesn't seem to exist when it comes to the jumping cholla cactus. It doesn't really jump but breaks off easily, if even lightly touched. And the fish-hook-like spines don't let go. During our recent travels, Charlize somehow knew to avoid getting close enough to that troublesome plant to experience it. And I don't recall treating the same dog more than once for a cholla encounter, so it must be worse than porcupines from a dog's perspective.

Charlize does love to chase small creatures, though. She has come amazingly close but has yet to capture one. And we haven't run into a porcupine ... yet.

27

Contemplating Laziness

Only in laziness can we achieve a state of contemplation which is a balancing of values, a weighing of oneself against the world and the world against itself ... We do not think a lazy man can commit murders... And a nation of lazy contemplative men would be incapable of fighting a war unless their very laziness were attacked.

John Steinbeck
The Log from the Sea of Cortez

WHEN I WAS STILL INVOLVED IN ACADEMIC LIFE, as a department head, my waking hours and, even some sleeping hours, were dominated by deadlines: deadlines for grant proposals, deadlines for a myriad of administrative details, deadlines for articles to submit to scientific journals, deadlines to review others' papers for those journals, deadlines to prepare for classes and exams, deadlines for reviewing grant applications for National Institute of Health study sections, deadlines for budgets, for reports, for meeting with and advising students ... Well, you get the idea. Lots of deadlines. I was a busy person. Busy in the classroom, busy in my lab, busy in my offices, both at the university and at home. There was always something that needed to be finished, deadlines to meet.

Charlize busily, not lazily, carrying her ball at the dog beach.

After I retired, Rosalie insisted that I cultivate some laziness. The problem is that I'm easily bored. So after moving to the Seattle area to be closer to our two sons and their families, I renovated the house we bought, finished the third edition of my reference textbook, started writing fiction, and took up fly-fishing again after a fifty-year hiatus. I'm still a busy person.

Lately I've started paying close attention to the way Charlize lives her life. She doesn't have any deadlines but is insistent about her two constitutional walks a day. As I pick up after her and carry the biodegradable green bags as we continue her walk, I wonder who, exactly, is in charge. What would a visitor from another planet think our pecking order is? But that's a whole other subject to contemplate.

Each day, Charlize plays fetch with me for ten or fifteen minutes, eats what I put in front of her when I put it down, asks to be petted from time to time, and is either fast asleep or dozing at least twenty hours every day. Her only responsibilities are to comfort and guard me. I think she has the whole lazy thing figured out. She's unlikely to start a war but will steal the treats from my jacket pocket if I leave it where she can get to them.

28

GOING FISHING

CHARLIZE AND I WENT FISHING at Lenice Lake, just south and east of where I-90 crosses the Columbia River in south-central Washington. It's a small lake set in a desert of almost brown sand, similarly colored rocks, sagebrush, and little else. The area does have a stark sort of beauty, but the boat launch is more than a quarter of a mile from the gravel parking lot that also serves as a bare-bones campground. It's a long way to push a pontoon boat on one wheel. But it's worth it. The lake is reported to be one of the best early-spring catch-and-release fly-fishing lakes in the state.

We arrived Friday evening with a couple of hours of daylight remaining. After I set up Frog, Charlize and I walked to where the cattails had been removed to provide access to the water. The lake was roiling with whitecaps.

Charlize immediately waded out into the lake to greet a couple of fishermen who were bringing their pontoon boats into the landing. After petting Charlize, they reported reasonable fishing success given the windy conditions. They showed me the egg pattern they were using and even gave me one yellow fly and one orange fly to try out. My experience with the catch-and-release fraternity is that they are almost always willing to share their techniques and strategies. My two new friends even described their technique for tying the flies. My guess is that since members of this fraternity release everything they catch, there's no competition with other people fishing. Any fish there are available for everyone.

Hope is the mantra of any person sitting in a boat on a lake or standing in a stream, especially if the wind is blowing the water into whitecaps. Anyone practicing catch-and-release fly-fishing has to believe that the next cast, the next self-tied fly will produce a result. Interestingly, the fraternity is no longer solely male. The gentle gender has discovered the joys of freezing cold water, windy days, rain, and uninterested trout. What the hell is the matter with them?

Saturday morning, while I fought whitecaps and wind on the lake, Charlize stayed inside in the warmth of Old Blue's covered bed. Meanwhile, I was trying the egg patterns and half a dozen other types of flies, different colors of leech patterns, and woolly buggers. I had one strike that I missed landing, and after another couple of hours without a single strike, I struggled to row back to the landing. I was rowing against the wind, a foot forward for every dozen strokes.

Eventually I arrived back at the parking lot and let Charlize out to run about. She soon found another friend and introduced me to him. He had access to a radio and told me the wind was forecast to continue through Sunday.

I gave up, hitched up Frog, and we headed home to Edmonds.

Rosalie never grasped the concept. "Let's see," she smirked, "you put on those wader thingies that you can't get off afterwards and the life jacket in case you fall in and the fishing vest loaded with all kinds of toys and goodies and the flippers that kill your ankles, and then you kick with those flippers or row around the lake while you sit in that float thingy in the cold water. You spend many hundreds of our dollars on equipment and more hours tying things onto hooks that don't resemble any bug I've ever seen, then drive for even more hours to get to a lake or river, and if you do catch a fish, you let it go. Have I left out anything?"

"You just don't understand," I responded.

29

ON THE ROAD AGAIN

As we pulled out of my driveway, I caught a glimpse of the sound and the sun glistening off the brilliant white snow topping the Olympics. I waved goodbye for however long it would be until Charlize and I would return home.

We traveled the same roads as we had on our trip to Lenice Lake, catching I-405 and then I-90 going east. At seven o'clock on Sunday morning, there wasn't much traffic. After crossing the Columbia River, we found Highway 26 and were in interesting new territory—lots of irrigated farmland, sprinklers moving sedately in huge half-circles blowing mist on green fields, and fruit orchards already past their bloom, now greening up.

Now in mid-day, the traffic going west was heavy on the two-lane road—many of the occupants probably parents returning to the Seattle area from their offspring's graduation at Washington State University. Most of the vehicles were filled with happy, smiling faces, but some faces sported frowns (maybe too much celebrating?). I wondered what life had in store for their recent graduates ...

My brunch in Colfax was a bad choice—a breakfast scramble with potatoes, sausage, ham, onions, green pepper, cheese, and some other stuff I couldn't identify. There was too much quantity, too many different ingredients, and way too much grease. I choked down as much as I could and took out the considerable remainder in a Styrofoam container, which I offered to Charlize in the back of Old Blue. My normally dainty-eating dog wolfed down the stuff—fast. What was that about?

I had planned to stop for the night in Lewiston, Idaho, but the weather was beautiful, the roads were mostly ours, and it was early. We pressed on to Idaho's Winchester Lake State Park, arriving about four o'clock in the afternoon. The lady at the gatehouse was pleasant, gentile, and apologetic as she explained the fee system. Since I didn't have an Annual Motor Vehicle Entrance Fee Sticker for Idaho and the one I have for Washington didn't count, I would have to dig up forty dollars, even for only one night. "But it will be good if you decide to return to any Idaho State Park during 2013," she explained. There also was a ten-dollar surcharge and $23.32 for a site with water and electricity, but nothing else. The place was nice, but not almost seventy-five-dollars nice! I decided to press on. The nice lady said she understood completely.

An unhappy Charlize because I stopped her from taking a dip in the Clearwater River—too fast for her.

We drove to Grangeville, Idaho, and found another RV resort. That night I sat at Frog's little dinette and looked west at a series of green pastures stretching to the mountains. Two horses were grazing in the nearest pasture—a healthy looking paint and an emaciated sorrel, bony hips, ribs showing, who appeared to be very old.

Charlize climbed up next to me on the bench. I put my arm around her and patted her. We watched the sun set beyond the mountains, backlighting them into a dark purple. A rose hue framed the stark peaks in silhouette. Charlize leaned against me and then stretched out on her side and put her muzzle in my lap, expecting to be petted. She manages to mirror my mood.

The next morning, we made our way to the Lewis and Clark Highway, traveling northeast following the Clearwater River through what my map declares to be a "wild and scenic river corridor." It's all of that and much more. Numerous historical markers describe events that took place during the Lewis and Clark expedition. There are also landmarks of the Nez Perce ("pierced nose"), the tribe that claimed the environs then and now and provided so much aid and comfort to the explorers and mountain men who followed, only to be repaid by horrendous crimes perpetrated against them, more of the effects of manifest destiny that I've written about.

30

On to Montana

Our second day out on the road again, we made some serious tracks. After experiencing the Lewis and Clark Trail, Charlize and I turned south to follow the Bitterroot River flowing north. We continued south past Sula and then turned east to cross over Chief Joseph Pass at 7,200 feet above sea level. We were at the northern edge of the Bitterroot Mountain range, where the Corps of Discovery had suffered so much on their way to the Columbia River. At the Lolo Summit, I let Charlize out, and she peed on both sides of the continental divide. Good dog!

We pressed on to the Big Hole National Battlefield site, where the Nez Perce tribe fought the 7th Infantry Regiment led by General Oliver O. Howard on August 9 and 10, 1877. That was the largest battle fought during what is called the Nez Perce War—a war that lasted five months.

The Nez Perce had made treaties with the US government in 1855 and again in 1863. Those treaties ensured that the tribe could stay on a small portion of its original lands, spanning parts of three current states. The much smaller parcel of land they were promised was in the Wallowa Valley along the Grande Ronde River in northeastern Oregon. In 1877, General Oliver was instructed to attack the tribe if it did not relocate to yet another, even smaller, reservation in Idaho. Chief Joseph reluctantly agreed, but three young braves, enraged by these machinations of the US government, massacred a band of white settlers who were moving into what was the tribe's original homeland.

Here's the plaque, to spare you a photo of Charlize doing her business.

To avoid further problems, Chief Joseph decided to move the tribe to Canada, but it was intercepted at Big Hole. The warriors fought a day-and-a-half, delaying action to allow as many women and children as possible to escape. By some accounts, at least ninety members of the tribe, mostly women and children, were killed. Twenty-eight of the US forces died, and forty were seriously wounded.

The delaying action did allow many of the tribe's members to escape. They continued their trek but were caught again in October, only forty miles from the Canadian border—and safety. By this time, the tattered survivors were starving and exhausted. Chief Joseph was forced to surrender to save those who had survived. About 150 tribal members who had gone ahead did make it to Canada prior to the surrender.

This history lesson was the depressing culmination of an otherwise amazing and inspiring full day. To wind down, we found an RV park in Wisdom, Montana, not far from the battlefield. Two trailers were parked there, but no occupants, and as long as Charlize and I were around, we didn't see another person in or around the place. A sign instructed prospective patrons to fill out the form on one of the envelopes provided, leave thirty dollars, and enjoy the facilities. There was an electric service box, and we plugged in, but the water was still turned off to prevent the water lines from freezing. There was no Wi-Fi, no cell phone service, no cable TV, and the door to the restroom/laundry was locked.

The good news was that less than a couple hundred yards away was Letty's bar/restaurant. Some vehicles were parked in front, indicating that a few patrons were inside—a good sign, considering the lack of human activity in the town otherwise. Two glasses of drinkable, but not memorable, red Zinfandel, made my dinner of a salad, a chewy steak, an over-baked potato, and a roll reasonably edible. I left half of everything except the Zinfandel for Charlize. I cut up the leftovers and mixed them with a cup of her kibble, and she again abandoned her normally dainty eating habits.

A bitter-cold early spring in Wisdom, Montana.

We went to bed early, so both Charlize and I were up at four thirty the next morning and on the road by five o'clock. The sky was starting to lighten, casting a red-tinged gray light on the mountains to the east. As we headed mostly in that direction, the increasing light reflected off the rock-induced waves and ripples of the fast-running Big Hole River to our left.

The Madison River Valley near Ennis, Montana, one of the world's most beautiful fly-fishing destinations.

Just as the sun peeked over the mountaintops and I started to lower Old Blue's visor, a cow moose loped across the road in front of us. I touched the brakes, but the moose was already safely distant and unconcerned. She made an effortless hop over a four-strand barbed-wire fence and continued nonplussed on her way toward the river. An excited Charlize barked her appreciation of this extraordinary feat.

Because of our early start, it was still before noon when we arrived at a nice, full-service RV park in Ennis, Montana. I shelled out another thirty dollars a night for two nights' stay, but everything was provided, and the restrooms and showers were new and immaculate.

After setting up Frog and detaching her from Old Blue, I checked in with the Madison River Fishing Company, where I met Matt, the fishing guide I had reserved for the next day's adventure. I told Matt that because it was so early in the day, I might want to do some bank or wade fishing. He told me where to go and sold me some flies that he thought might be productive.

Charlize was a pill. She considered my attempts at casting as playing retrieve with her. She followed the line into the water, barking her excitement. After repeated stern warnings to cease and desist, she completely ignored me. And she increased my irritation by snapping at the line or my fly rod with each new cast. I gave up and put her in Old Blue. She obviously didn't understand the reason for her imprisonment and considered it unfair.

After trying all the flies that Matt had sold me, plus some of my own that I had tied before leaving Edmonds, I managed to snag only some twigs hanging on a tree and some floating past in the water. The water was moving fast, and the rocky bottom was slippery, so after a half-hearted attempt with my bum ankle, I gave up wading and walked—actually limped—the bank with equal non-success. With the nonsensical optimism of a true amateur, I decided I'd do better the next day with Matt's tutoring and guidance.

31

FLY FISHING THE MADISON RIVER

As PROMISED, my hired fishing guide, Matt, called about six o'clock that evening to agree on the most propitious time to go out. After checking with his fishing-guide buddies, we decided that the following afternoon would be a good time to get into a Mayfly hatch and do some dry fly fishing. This would be an exciting new experience for me.

The next morning, Matt drove us upriver, where he put his float boat in the water and readied all the rods and other equipment. He watched me cast a few times on the bank, made some corrections in my technique, and we took off, accompanied by Charlize. We had talked about the wisdom of taking her in the boat, but Matt assured me that he takes his own dog with him when he goes fishing on his own, and he was certain Charlize would adjust.

Well, it was not to be. The first time I cast my line, Charlize jumped out of the boat into the river to go after it. Matt had rigged my rod with two different flies and an indicator, which we called bobbers when I was a lad. He explained that with the strong wind and swift current, the indicator would carry the bait downstream faster and I would be better able to mend and control the line. Okay ... whatever. He's the expert.

Charlize was convinced that the bobber/indicator was her ball, and she was determined to retrieve it, so the pantomime continued. Matt and I took turns hauling Charlize back into the fast-moving boat. Losing patience, I took her leash and snubbed her tight to the swivel chair on which I was sitting.

Every time I cast, she barked incessantly and, by swiveling my chair, managed to gain enough slack to lunge after the bobber when it hit the water. I lost all patience with her, but Matt was calm and understanding. After all, he was getting paid, no matter how stupid his client and his dog were acting. After many of my loud corrections, Charlize finally calmed down and behaved—or maybe she just got tired of the game she was enjoying a lot more than I was.

As we drifted in the fast current, Matt instructed me on where to cast and how to "mend" the line. Before long, I hooked, and Matt netted, a ten-inch-long whitefish, cousin to the trout and native to the Madison. The next fish netted was also a whitefish, then a nice rainbow trout, maybe fourteen inches long and heavy. All were returned, unharmed, to the water.

A German brown joining the other catches back in the river.

Matt showing off the biggest fish caught on a spectacular day.

Not long after that, I landed two or three small rainbows, new plants, and I didn't even need net. I put them back in the water to grow. A nice-sized German brown trout, also native to the river, was netted, photographed, and turned loose. On the next cast, I got another rainbow. When I was fighting to bring in a fish, and even after they were netted, Charlize seemed uninterested, even bored—quite an about-face from her original excitement. Matt told me his dog goes nuts when he brings in a fish.

After almost five hours of sun, fun, fast water, and memorable fishing, we reached the pullout. A compatriot of Matt's had retrieved Matt's vehicle and trailer and parked it at the pullout site. My face and hands were sunburned, but it was a fantastic day on a world-renowned river, spectacular scenery, and damned if I didn't catch some fish. And I have the photos to prove it.

To celebrate, I bought a couple of beers for Matt and myself at his favorite watering hole. We rehashed a day that I will always consider outstanding but he considered "about average."

The previous evening, I had connected with Dan at the RV Park while he was walking his miniature schnauzer and I was walking Charlize. Charlize made a new friend, and Dan and I learned that we were both recently widowed after long marriages. We were both doing our best to try to learn how to manage on our own and agreed to go out for dinner together after my fishing outing the next day.

After such a successful day, I was ready for a good meal. We went to the local bowling alley, where Dan had been told the food was very good. To my great surprise, it actually was; a bowling alley is not a place I would expect gourmet food to be served. We talked for some time over dinner and discovered that we were kindred spirits.

Chapter 32

Yellowstone Park Revisited

It never occurred to me that visiting Yellowstone again would be so difficult. In my book, *Animals Don't Blush*, I recounted the camping adventures that Rosalie and I experienced immediately after my graduation from vet school. Our travels combined Rosalie's first experience with camping, our honeymoon, and arriving at my first veterinary job in Sidney, Montana. That trip took place during the first week in June of 1960. We were on a tight schedule, but Rosalie, my first German shepherd, Mister, and I spent two days in Yellowstone Park. I considered the entire experiences an adventure. Rosalie used other, less positive descriptors.

Now, decades later, Charlize and I came in from the town of West Yellowstone. I was appalled at the destruction and at the same time amazed at the recovery following the forest fires of 1988. Almost eight hundred thousand acres (more than three thousand square kilometers), about 36 percent of the entire park, had been engulfed in flames.

We arrived early in the day, as it was only seventy-some miles from Ennis, Montana, to West Yellowstone. Once in the park, driving on roads that were significantly wider and better paved than they were in 1960, I kept glancing at the stark skeletons of once-proud trees, interspersed with a few fire-charred survivors, all engulfed in a sea of uniform-height young trees elbowing each other for space.

Uniform new growth after the 1988 forest fires in Yellowstone.

Some experts knew (many did not) that the lodgepole pine, dominant in Yellowstone, drops mostly closed pinecones that don't open to release their seeds until they're stimulated by intense heat. The forest floor was covered with these closed cones, accumulated over many years, and the fires must have moved swiftly enough to expose but not consume the seeds. Those seeds found conditions ideal for germination, and the result is thousands, maybe millions, of seven- to twelve-feet tall trees, obviously germinated at the same time. In the not too distant future, these saplings will have to cull themselves to obtain the required space and light to survive.

In 1960, we had had to progress on our way to Sidney, so each night I had set up the old canvas umbrella tent that had served my family for years. In early June of that year, Rosalie and I had been two of only a few occupants of Yellowstone's Madison Campground. In those days, gravel roads characterized the campground, and we had a handpump for water, outhouses, and in-the-ground garbage receptacles that did little to discourage bears.

Now, half a century later, Charlize and I set up Frog in the enlarged, updated, and improved Madison Campground, featuring paved roads, heated restrooms with running water, and flush toilets. This time, Charlize and I arrived during the first week in May, and some of the roads into the park were still closed, but the campground was at least a third full of people and their RVs.

After Frog was situated, I disconnected Old Blue, and Charlize and I went to visit Old Faithful. The amount and character of new development and the number of people, some arriving in busloads so early in the season, was astounding—nay depressing. I couldn't ignore those memories of our significantly different visit fifty-plus years previous.

Rosalie and I made a habit of not revisiting places we had been to, and thus no return to Yellowstone. There were always new places to visit and explore, and my profession took us to many of them, mostly on somebody else's dime. We visited a lot of new places in the United States, Mexico, and Europe.

Those trips made great memories, and travel disasters make the best stories.

One of our wedding gifts was an eight-millimeter movie camera. On our trip to Yellowstone, we took endless footage of scenery, "wild" animals, geysers, steam rising from the ground, and bubbling cauldrons of mud. After watching those boring films once or twice, we rarely looked at them again. But a few years ago, I was worried about losing the films to age, so I converted them to videotape and some years later to CDs. They're painful to watch, but not nearly as painful as revisiting those places without my bride.

Charlize didn't enjoy Yellowstone at all. Nowadays, there are rules, lots of rules, concerning dogs. Dogs must be on a leash at all times and can't be taken out of the confines of the campground or parking lots. We can't leave them alone tied up. Naturally, we have to pick up after our dogs. I understand the need for all those rules. Too many people with too many dogs, and the dogs could get into trouble with wildlife and cause other types of ecological problems, but the last time I was here with Rosalie and Mister, and Mister was a hero of a dog. (You'll have to read *Animals Don't Blush* to find out how and why.) Mister was always under voice control and off-leash. By comparison, Charlize's demeanor in the photo says it all.

No fun for Charlize, limiting where she could go.

Frog's many energy-consuming appliances sucked her battery dry by nine o'clock at night. The Madison Campground still lacks electrical and water hookups, but I presume those will come eventually. Frog's smoke alarm beeped once a minute to let me know the battery was low, but there was enough juice to keep the damn thing beeping until one o'clock in the morning. I got into bed when the power gave out at nine o'clock, but, of course, the beeping didn't let me get to sleep until it finally ran out of juice.

I woke up at six o'clock, got my clothes on in the freezing cold—no power, no functioning furnace–and made a dash to the heated restroom. Our two sons and I used to do a lot of backpacking, frequently in cold weather, but we were equipped and dressed to handle it. Frog has the comforts of home, so when the power goes out, a warm restroom with a flush toilet on a cold morning has definite appeal.

After returning from the restroom, I took Charlize for her walk and then hooked up Frog to Old Blue, so now there was power from the truck's battery. I boiled water and made coffee and some instant oatmeal, fed Charlize, took her for another walk, and by seven o'clock, we were on our way to the east gate.

The sage saying that you can't go back was correct. Too much change, too many memories. Going back to Yellowstone was a mistake. Tomorrow, we'll arrive at Pass Ranch in the Sandhills of Nebraska. That will be moving forward.

33

THE PASS RANCH

WHEN I WAS FIRST A STUDENT at what was then Colorado A & M, in 1954, the freshmen were assigned to Green Hall. My room was across the hall from Don's, and neither of us cared much for our assigned roommates. I have no recollection of how we managed it, but by the second term, we were rooming together.

The short, slight rancher's son, who grew up in the wilds of the Sandhills of Nebraska, and the tall Jewish swimmer from Phoenix, Arizona, seemed like an unlikely pair. We were nicknamed Mutt and Jeff, of course, but we found an abundance of common interests. We had both grown up with taciturn fathers who rarely talked unless they were giving instructions or needed to say something important. We both loved our dads and were comfortable being with them all day without talking. Considering that background, Don and I were never uncomfortable being together without talking, and that remains true to this day, although we frequently find plenty to talk about.

After that first year, we shared an apartment with two other friends, and the third year, my first in veterinary school, we shared a small house with two third-year veterinary students. In all that time as roommates, I can't recall a single argument between us.

I was far from my folk's home in Phoenix, and Don's ranch was only a long day's drive from Fort Collins. Don had a car, and he invited me to spend Thanksgiving at the ranch the first year. His folks were warm and welcoming, especially his mom. That holiday was memorable as my first experience on a working commercial ranch. For several years thereafter, I was invited and went there and always felt welcome. I felt then, and still do today, that the Pass Ranch is my second home.

Over the years, Don and I have stayed in sporadic touch. He graduated with a degree in agricultural economics and returned to the same ranch that his great-grandfather started and his grandfather and then his dad continued to operate. He got married, I got married, and—miracle of miracles—our wives Susie and Rosalie became close friends. Don gradually took over the operation of the ranch from his dad.

The sign at the front entrance to Pass Ranch. The other ranch on the sign is directly west of Don's Pass Ranch and formerly belonged to his uncle. Jim Hanna was Don and Susie's deceased eldest son who was taking over, long tragic story.

When we lived in Montana, Don and Susie visited us, and after we moved to Phoenix, the visits continued sporadically. They also visited us when we lived in Illinois. We visited them at their ranch several times, and sometimes we met where it was convenient to all. Each time we got together, we picked up as though we had been together the day before, despite the passage of years.

At the ranch, Charlize thought she was in heaven. She stayed close to me in the house, but outside, she was beckoned by thousands of acres to roam and hundreds of wild critters, as well as cows, calves, steers, bulls, and horses, to discover. She didn't wander too far, though, and kept looking back to make certain I didn't leave without her.

Mother cows with their calves on the hill pasture.

Cattle on the hill were brought down to the hay meadow close to the house.

34

THE SANDHILLS

THE SANDHILLS ARE JUST THAT—hills of sand and valleys of sand and hollows of sand—all held in place by a sod formed by the roots and stems of a wide variety of native grasses. If the grasses are destroyed by fire or by too much traffic from cattle or vehicles or a myriad of other possibilities, the result is a "blowout," a spot where the sand is exposed to the wind and occasional rain. A miniature sand-dune desert evolves.

In the late 1800s and early 1900s, sections of land, 640-acre plots in the Sandhills, were made available for homesteading. A community of black families settled on portions of what eventually became the Pass Ranch. The new settlers plowed the prairie and were fortunate to have abnormally high amounts of rain for a time, but the inevitable came to pass (pun intended). With normal amounts of rain, or less, there were no more crops, just sand dunes. Most of the farms were in dire straits when my friend Don's great-grandfather showed up and offered what everyone considered a fair price under the circumstances. Putting these properties together with the purchase of adjacent rangelands, he built essentially the same ranch that Don now operates.

Don working on one of the gates. There was about two feet of open space from the bottom wire to the ground where the ground (sand) had eroded—plenty of room for a calf to slip under the wire.

Now it's fixed.

*Here is a water tank that needed work with a
blowout in the background.*

Don and I, with Charlize following along, rode in one of the ranch pickups through various pastures checking on the welfare of cattle divided into various groups—young bulls, old bulls, replacement heifers, first-calf heifers with their calves, cows with their calves, steers growing to be sold early this coming fall, and heifers recently separated for sale. The groups were parceled out in various pastures, some further divided and scattered to take advantage of whatever early pasture grass was available.

The ranch is roughly shaped like the state of Kentucky, the fat section, with most of the ranch buildings to the east and narrowing to the west. It is divided into pastures and meadows for haying. Most take up roughly six hundred acres. Some are purposely smaller and consist of hills and small valleys. The flat valley sections are used as hay meadows. We drove slowly. Charlize was loping alongside the pickup, her tongue lolling first to one side then the other. Don pointed out sites of some of the old homesteads. One of them had foundation stones scattered in a small hollow where the house, long gone, had stood. The stones had to have been hauled a long distance by horse and wagon. We covered a couple of miles before Charlize started to lag and was happy to join us in the cab after having refused to get in when we started out. Anyway, she would be in shape when we'd leave if she kept this up.

A few years ago, the relatives of one of the black homesteaders showed up at the ranch, tracing their family's history. There are a lot of stories to be told about those intrepid settlers and what happened to those families. If I live long enough, maybe I'll get to them, if someone else doesn't do it first.

That afternoon Don drove a large tractor to scrape out sod from a nearby site and then filled the eroded spots. My job was to follow him in a pickup to the next pasture that needed work, open gates for him to drive the tractor through, and then close the gate behind us. We needed the four-wheel-drive pickup to get back to the house, an hour's drive away, on dirt tracks and across the pastures and hills.

35

FULL WORKING DAY ON PASS RANCH

LAST YEAR, ONLY A LITTLE MORE than seven inches of rain fell on the ranch, the driest year since Don's great-granddad put the property together and the family started keeping records. And this past winter, there wasn't as much moisture as usual, although a blizzard in late April helped somewhat. But the blizzard came during calving season, and some calves were lost. Recounting this, Don just shrugged and told me that accepting whatever nature provides, good or bad, is just another part of coping with the long list of things you have no control over and have to deal with in the ranching life.

"There's no such thing as an average year," Don said. "Every year brings a different set of problems to cope with. May is supposed to be cold and wet, but this year it's warm and dry." Again he shrugged.

Our early morning started with the TV turned to the weather report as usual. Today the forecast was for temperatures in the nineties, possibly a record high for mid-May. All the pastures were brown and dry, and even the meadows in the valleys were late to green and grow.

Before our arrival, Don and his crew cut out forty heifers from the two hundred he saved as replacements to be bred this year. He wasn't certain if there would be sufficient rain to provide enough good-quality hay and pasture to take all of his animals through next winter. If the females weren't going to produce a calf next spring or if he didn't have enough feed to grow the steers to yearlings, he couldn't keep them.

The day before, I had gone with Don to feed "cake," a pellet form of protein supplement made from corn and soybeans with minerals and vitamins and other ingredients. We went to three different pastures in one of his three-quarter-ton flatbed pickups with a large hopper on the bed filled with the cake. In one of the pastures, we fed the culled heifers to put some additional weight on them before selling them.

We pulled into a pasture holding several young bulls. Don pulled a knob on the dash, and a siren wailed, telling the animals he was there with treats. When they all arrived, a couple of them rubbed themselves on the truck. Then Don drove in a circle, metering and spreading the cake on the ground. When the prescribed amount was deposited, he got out, closed the trap door, and we were off to the next group to be fed.

Charlize was with us, supervising, getting in shape.

The first time I visited the Pass Ranch, Thanksgiving holiday in 1954, we loaded large sacks, probably sixty or seventy pounds each, maybe more, into the bed of a pickup, then drove to the pastures, honked the horn to call the cattle, and then had to open each sack and walk with it to meter out the cake. This way is a lot easier.

Don and Susie's house.

Sunday afternoon, we did upkeep and maintenance chores on Don and Susie's house, originally built in the early 1900s and remodeled several times. All the buildings, except the equipment barns, were made of wood siding, and in the extreme weather of the Sandhills, the buildings have to be repainted on a regular basis. Oh yes—all the pastures and meadows had at least one windmill with a stock tank, and the large pastures had two or more. A lot of maintenance.

36

A Mile High

Taking a break from ranch life, Charlize and I made the six-hour drive to Denver to revisit old friends and spend some time in the Mile High City. This spring was late in coming to the eastern slope and western plains—late snows and cold. Charlize and I arrived in mid-May, when the trees were just starting to leaf out. The tulips were spreading their splashes of color, and the peony buds were opening. Bright red-orange poppies were common in the front gardens of the neighborhood of my friend Lou, who I stayed with.

His house, a brick Craftsman style, was built in the early 1900s. The original owner, legend says, was a gangster. The house is only a block away from Cheesman Park, which has lots of grass, lots of trees around the border, lots of open space, and lots of dogs walking their servants. (I presume those folks walking behind with bags of poop deposited by the dogs are servants. What else could they be?) Sadly there's no off-leash area for the dogs. Charlize was okay with the place, but it wasn't Pass Ranch.

My host wanted to have a dinner party for old mutual friends, and I decided to cook because I felt guilty about mooching off friends for so long. I prepared the dinner that Rosalie and I saved for special occasions:

my famous veal chops Marsala with a breadcrumb topping, braised with shallots and mushrooms, and then baked. It was accompanied by spinach pasta dressed with ricotta, Parmigiano-Reggiano cheese, and butter, and roasted fresh asparagus. One of our guests brought the wine.

For dessert, Rosalie always baked something special for these events, and she was awesome with pies, especially if we had fresh rhubarb in the garden. I don't bake, and neither does my host, so we wimped out and purchased a nice-looking peach tart at Tony's.

Everyone at the dinner knew Rosalie. Lou is a talker and brilliant at controlling conversations. Whenever tears came to my eyes, he quickly redirected the conversation.

Yes, I still miss her, especially at night. Sleeping alone in a king-sized bed after more than fifty-two years with a partner is still difficult. I doubt I'll ever get used to it, but the days are getting easier. Charlize continues to stay close to me wherever I go, day and night, and each morning, she still nudges me with her cold nose to get up. If I don't get up immediately, she puts a paw on the mattress close to my face. That elicits an irritated response from me. No dogs allowed on the furniture, and especially not on the bed, but it has the effect she desires. I'm up.

While out and about, walking with some of my Denver friends on our way to a restaurant for dinner one night, I glanced in a storefront window as we passed by. All of us were dressed like the old people we are. The men were in flannel shirts, jeans, and walking shoes—or, in my case, hiking boots to support my arthritic ankle. The women were attired in loose-fitting pants in a variety of dark colors and coordinated pullover tops. All of us were overweight, to a greater or lesser extent, and all of us were limping, but from different causes: knees, hips, ankles, and/or backs. One friend was pushing a walker. Got the picture yet?

Last week, another of our veterinary school classmates passed away. What a mess life is! The good news is that we can still get around. We still can drink a little wine, enjoy good food, visit with old friends, and laugh. We *do* laugh about shared memories and the sorry state of a world in which we are no longer the movers and shakers (if we ever were). Laughing about our aches and pains seems to lessen our woes. I have a feeling that when we can no longer laugh, the whole thing will be over with.

37

RETURN TO DENVER

SEEMS I CAN'T STAY AWAY FROM DENVER. I went back to visit those
old friends who have made a special effort to welcome and include
me in their lives, even after a fifty-plus year hiatus of minimal contact.
I knew some of them back when CSU was still Colorado A & M and
we were all young and unbelievably ignorant of life.

Denver has become a cosmopolitan city, and my friends participate
in many of the activities that made it so—live operas from the MET,
projected live to a big-screen movie theater, professional sports, high-
end dining experiences; you get the idea. When I visited, their lives
seemed so different from mine in quiet, artsy Edmonds, but I'm certain
I couldn't live in that environment fulltime. I've come to rely on the
moist air, overcast days, and lush green—not to mention my eldest son
and his family, who I already missed after only twelve days away from
them. Still, the high desert is a great place to visit. Maybe I'm destined
to just wander and then return to Edmonds only to wander again. Not
so terrible a thing to contemplate.

Although I looked forward to seeing my host, I was a little apprehensive about Charlize meeting his new dog, Chloe, a Maltese/Pomera-
nian that might weigh five pounds before shaking off her bath water.
Charlize had developed some troubling behavior a while back. When
on leash, she was extremely aggressive to other dogs when encountering

them while out walking. I started using the techniques promulgated by the Dog Whisperer on his TV show, and we made good progress. If I spotted another dog, before we were too close, I put Charlize in a "sit" and made her pay attention to me. This prevented her from getting her ruff up, snarling and lunging at the other dog. What is remarkable about this aggressive behavior is that when I took her to an off-leash dog park, she wasn't aggressive to the other dogs at all.

Anyway, when we introduced Charlize and Chloe to each other, I put Charlize in a "down stay." She wagged her entire hind end, and although Chloe was a little apprehensive and slightly aggressive at first, they started getting along with no problems and even playing together when the spirit moved them. Chloe hid under a chair or couch where Charlize couldn't reach her and then launched preemptive strikes, followed by a quick retreat to safety. Chloe seemed almost cat-like in her ability to instantaneously regain her balance, change directions in the air, and leap onto surfaces twice her height.

Charlize seemed mostly bemused at this behavior but seemed to be getting the idea that it was a game. Occasionally, she responded and landed one of her big paws, knocking Chloe off balance, but only for an instant. All was forgiven. To cement their friendship, she and Charlize shared a plate of leftover quiche. Fun to watch.

Charlize's friend Chloe protecting her spot on the couch.

I went online and found an off-leash dog park not too far from Lou's home. Charlize and I went there several times. One morning by seven o'clock, it was already in the high eighties, and the forecast was for the temperature to reach the mid-nineties with bright sunshine and clear air in the high altitude. A dozen or more dogs and their people were already in the park when we arrived shortly after eight o'clock.

Charlize was completely focused on her ball racing after it each time I threw it, and I threw it as hard and far as I could, using the plastic Chuckit stick. She ignored the other dogs, and even if she wasn't the fastest, she was the most focused, almost always ending up with her own ball. She ignored the other dogs, holding the ball in her mouth until she caught her breath before dropping it for me to throw it again. When the other dog owners threw a ball for their dogs, or if they intercepted Charlize's ball and threw it out, she ignored it. It had to be her ball, and I had to be the person throwing it for her to play the game. While she brought the ball back, she continued to ignore the other dogs, even when they tried to interfere with her progress back to me. She showed no aggressive behavior in response to the challenges by any of the other dogs. Good girl!

38

GREAT FALLS OF THE MISSOURI

A s an enthusiast of all things related to the Lewis and Clark expedition, I was intrigued reading about the many extraordinary obstacles they overcame during their journey—including the portage of the Great Falls of the Missouri River. Never having been there, I wanted to experience these wonders of nature firsthand. So on our trip home from Denver, Charlize and I made a detour to Great Falls, Montana.

Lewis and Clark anticipated finding these falls, which the Mandan tribe of Native Americans had described during the winter of 1804. As he frequently did, Lewis left the party with Clark in charge of continuing the struggle to move all their supplies and equipment westward against the current of the river on June 13 of 1805. After Lewis had traveled about two miles, he heard the sound and saw the spray from the falls, and seven miles later, he arrived. Nobody could describe it better than he did in his journal, as edited by Elliott Coues in *The History of the Lewis and Clark Expedition* (Dover Publications, Inc., New York, reprint of the 1893 edition).

Briefly, Lewis described a cascade about three hundred yards wide with a hundred-foot cliff on the right side as he faced the falls. From the left cliff, the water fell for about eighty feet in one smooth sheet of water. The rest of the falling water crashed into a series of rocks creating a white foam extending about two hundred yards and rising an impressive eighty feet above the river. Columns of spray fifteen to twenty feet tall rose from the turbulent cascade catching the sun's rays and creating a bright rainbow. Below the falls, the river swiftly surged onward.

The next day, Lewis continued upstream and discovered a second falls, nineteen feet high and three hundred yards across, and named it Crooked Falls. Then he climbed a nearby hill and found a third waterfall that he described as "one of the most beautiful objects in nature, a cascade of about fifty feet perpendicular." Lewis named these falls the Beautiful Cascade, now known at Rainbow Falls. Farther upstream, Lewis spotted yet another falls only about six feet high but stretching more than a quarter of a mile across the river, and these became known as Colter Falls. He continued his explorations, and about two and a half miles upstream of Colter Falls, he located a fifth cataract, about twenty-six feet high and close to six hundred yards wide, which became known as Black Eagle Falls.

With Lewis's description in mind, Charlize and I eagerly looked forward to visiting these falls. What we found just upstream of the Great Falls was the Ryan Dam, which has reduced the Missouri River's flow to slightly more than a trickle. No roar, no mist, no rainbows. Between Rainbow Falls and the Great Falls resides the Cochrane Dam. And just downstream from Rainbow Falls is the Rainbow Dam, significantly reducing the flow over Crooked Falls. Colter Falls, upstream of the Rainbow Dam, is now submerged. The Black Eagle Falls are upstream of Black Eagle Dam, and the water held back by this structure has made the Black Eagle Falls a vestige of what the Corps of Discovery experienced. Damn, damn, damn.

The Great Falls of the Missouri River today.

The people now inhabiting the city and environs surely have benefitted from the hydroelectric power generated and the water impounded by these dams. That's progress. But just as it was impossible to experience the agonies of the Corps of Discovery's portage around the falls as described in the journals, it is no longer possible to experience the magnificence of those five cascades.

Charlize and I both considered the experience a bummer! She was and is very quick to sense my mood and responded by paying closer attention to me and staying very close, even leaning against me.

39

DISTURBING VULNERABILITY

Again, Charlize and I returned from Pass Ranch to my house with the peekaboo view of Puget Sound. I still felt Rosalie's presence in the house, but it was not as strong as it was prior to the start of this most recent trip. When Charlize and I returned from my first visit to Denver, I was pulling Frog through some blustery late-May weather with high winds and driving rain. That was adventuresome. It was also tiring, intense, and exhausting. That trip started me having second thoughts about the whole RV thing.

But to the issue at hand: I was educated about food-borne diseases and public health in veterinary school. We learned how to identify potential problems and how to prevent them because veterinarians play an important role in protecting our food supply. Food poisoning was something that happened to other people, not to me and not to my family.

Wrong! I had no recollection of hearing anything about *Campylobacter* back when I was in veterinary school. Now, however, I know a lot about *Campylobacter jujuni* and *coli*, the two most common causes of diarrheal illness in the United States, first described in 1963, after I graduated. These organisms are estimated to affect more than a million people each year, mostly during the summer months.

This is the view from Charlize's west-facing deck.

Two to five days after exposure, vulnerable people experience severe diarrhea, cramping, and abdominal pain with or without fever, nausea, vomiting—nice, eh? The symptoms usually last about a week and most commonly resolve themselves without treatment—except when they don't. Exposure is most commonly from infected poultry or produce but can occur from unpasteurized dairy products, contaminated water, or foodstuffs, and even from contact with feces from an infected pet. Back in 2011, an agency of the US government purchased raw chicken from a wide variety of grocery stores across the country. After testing those samples, 47 percent were found to be positive for the bacteria. That's a scary statistic.

Because I thought I just had a case of intestinal flu, I treated myself with several commonly used antidiarrheal agents. But after five days, I had lost twenty-five pounds with no improvement in the severe diarrhea. On the sixth day, I was feeling too weak to drive. My son responded to my call for help and drove me to the emergency room.

I was severely dehydrated. After the blood work was completed, the ER physician estimated that I was down to 10 percent or less of kidney function and in acute renal failure. Three days of hospitalization, intravenous fluids, and treatment for the bacterial culprit brought me around, but it was a close call. Another day or two and I would have been a candidate for kidney dialysis, maybe permanently.

The lesson learned is that at my reasonably advanced age, any illness can turn serious. I'm old enough to be vulnerable to a lot of things. The problem is that I don't feel any different than I did when I was fifty or even forty and still think I can respond to illnesses the same way I did then—by ignoring them. I have to get over that attitude.

During my hospital ordeal, Charlize spent three days with my son's family. After she rejoined me, she was unusually aware and sensitive, frequently coming over to check on me, staying close by, and insistent about being petted. Dogs can smell things such as uremia, and my blood urea nitrogen, one of the kidney function parameters, was still slightly above the normal range. Charlize sensed that all wasn't normal with me.

I have no idea what I ate that caused this problem. I hadn't handled or cooked any poultry product for some time, and Charlize wasn't showing any signs of a digestive disturbance, so the culprit wasn't exposure to her feces. The only thing I can think of was that I ate a lot of cherries shortly before feeling the first effects of the food poisoning. I had washed them, as I always do, but maybe not well enough. Some evidence indicates that ordinary rinsing with cold water may not be enough to wash off *Campylobacter*.

Anyhow, for people of an age—you're vulnerable. Be aware! Pets are also susceptible to this type of food poisoning, usually from infected raw poultry. Enough said about that. More than two days of non-responsive diarrhea and you, or your pet, need to be seen and your stool tested for this or some other equally dangerous disease. Dehydration and kidney failure are serious issues, and I learned my lesson.

40

CHARLIZE, CHLOE,
AND ME STILL GRIEVING

CHARLIZE'S NEW BUDDY CHLOE came along when my Denver friend Lou accompanied me from Denver to Edmonds in Old Blue (I made this trip to Denver minus Frog). He said that Chloe weighs five pounds, but I doubt if she tips the scales at much more than four pounds. On the way back to Edmonds, we visited Mount Rushmore, Great Falls, and other interesting spots along the way. The bond between the two dogs grew.

Charlize and Chloe played well together, but Charlize did reveal some jealousy. After we arrived at my place, the two of them invented a game involving one of Chloe's toys, a hollow rubber ball with another squeaky ball inside. Chloe would grab the ball and run all around my house, daring Charlize to take it from her, hiding under chairs and beds so Charlize couldn't reach her. Eventually, she would come out, and Charlize would corner her and take possession and then tease her by retiring to her own bed and pretending that she didn't want the ball but snatching it up again when Chloe got close.

Chloe left, and Charlize usurped her bed.

After their vacation with me ended and Chloe and Lou flew back to Denver, Charlize became quiet, almost depressed. I also became depressed—but for a different reason: After eight months of procrastination, I couldn't put it off any longer and started removing Rosalie's clothes from the four closets they occupied and bagging them up for transport to a charity that would put them to good use. She was a discerning shopper and purchased good stuff but rarely got rid of anything. I found some clothes I remember her wearing in the 1970s. She must have thought that she would be able to fit into them and/or the styles would regain their popularity. In any case, it wasn't an easy chore, but one I had to face.

My oldest son came over, and we had a long talk about how difficult it was for me to get rid of her clothes. He confessed that he still had emotional problems when he and his family visited me here—too much of his mother still in the house. He's still grieving, too. When does it become easier?

41

CHARLIZE'S NEW TRICK

THE GROSS FAMILY GATHERED for a family reunion at the Chevy Chase Cabins overlooking Discovery Bay on the Olympic Peninsula for a week. My brother and his wife came from Phoenix. My brother's son and his family, who live in Germany, joined us, along with my two sons and their families.

My older son and his family and his cousin from Germany and his family occupied the old original house. I stayed in a small cabin. My brother and his wife occupied another small cabin. My younger son and his family took over a second house. We gathered for all meals in the large house, sharing meal planning and preparation. It was great fun for all of us, and Charlize had a good time playing with the grand-daughters and grandnieces.

A deli lunch, catch-as-catch-can, nobody going hungry.

One morning, I went outside and saw my ten-year-old granddaughter and nine-year-old grandniece playing tetherball with Charlize. Well, it was quite a sight to witness, and I managed to record a video of it on my cell phone. I naively thought it was unique so I posted it on YouTube. I soon discovered that there are a lot of other videos of dogs playing tetherball already posted on that site. I suppose there is nothing new under the sun. Still, the video is fun to watch.

Charlize playing tetherball.

42

GETTING A HEADSTONE

IT WAS TIME TO DO SOMETHING about getting a headstone for Rosalie. It seems like nothing about losing a loved one is easy, simple, or straightforward. Eight months after her passing, I finally felt capable of dealing with this last—I hoped—detail. So I made some phone calls and found out what had to be done.

The first thing I needed was the name of a reliable place to purchase the stone. I chose from two suggested options and drove to the store to pick out a stone that would serve for both of us. My resting place will be on the same side of Rosalie as the way we slept for close to fifty-three years.

The first hitch in the process was that the place that sells the stones and carves the inscription doesn't sell stones directly to the public for people buried in the cemetery where Rosalie rests. I found out I would have to transact the purchase through the cemetery.

After another phone call, I arranged a time to meet with the manager of the cemetery at his office. When I showed up, he handed me two books. One was full of various designs and fonts for the inscription, and the other was replete with various symbols to adorn the stone—way too many choices. Eventually, I just did it. Rosalie won't know, and I was beyond caring about this task.

But I wasn't done here. I had to make decisions about how I wanted our names inscribed. Should I have them use Rosalie's full middle name or just her initial? Should I use her actual given name, Rose, or use Rosalie? She disliked her given name. Should I use her maiden name?

The cemetery manager could see that I was struggling and getting more upset the more I struggled. I supposed that I wasn't the first person he had shepherded through this process.

"Don't worry," he assured me. "Just put it in the way you are most happy with today. I'll send you a draft of what it will all look like, and you can discuss it with your family and make changes any time before they actually carve it."

Next we went to the gravesite to make certain the manager would place the stone correctly—and to make yet another decision: I had to choose between a concrete base and a granite base for the stone to be set on. He showed me an older grave where the concrete base was starting to disintegrate and one of about the same age where the granite was still pristine. Okay, at this point why not spend another several hundred dollars for the granite base?

During all the weeks following Rosalie's death, I visited her grave only three times before now. On those visits, I saw that the replaced turf had not taken hold and her gravesite was clearly visible. After a wet spring and mild summer, I wasn't prepared to see the struggling, brown-tinged turf that still clearly delineated her grave. I apologized to Rosalie silently but communicated my disappointment and displeasure to the manager aloud.

Throughout all this, Charlize waited in the back of Old Blue. When we finally got home, she knew I was upset and stayed very close, trying to let me know she was there for me and that everything would work out.

Rosalie often complained that I didn't talk to her enough. Now I find myself talking to her presence in the house while Charlize cocks her head and listens intently but without judgment. I feel as if Rosalie is more of a presence in our house than she is in that small plot of ground. I apologized again for the sad state of her grave and promised her I would make certain that unseemly situation was rectified.

I'm still searching for even a shred of humor in all of this. But it had to be done.

43

THE ROAD HOME

CHARLIZE AND I WERE ON THE ROAD AGAIN. This time we left Frog at home since the plan was to spend two weeks visiting my son and his family in their beautiful new home in Carlsbad, California. Rosalie would have loved their new house, especially the private guest room with en suite bath, the backyard saltwater pool with hot tub spilling into the pool, and the Mediterranean landscaping of the yard and neighborhood. Everything is idyllic.

The trip south from Edmonds was made in two and a half days. We buzzed down I-5 in Old Blue, fast but boring, even though the drive was a new one for us. Freeway speeds and heavy traffic don't equate to enjoyment of the experience, at least not for me. Charlize was just happy to be on the road again.

After our stay was over, we left early Sunday morning and managed to clear the Los Angeles traffic before eight. At Santa Clarita, we left the I-5 and worked our way west to US 101 and Santa Paula. Then we headed north along the coast. At about ten o'clock in the morning, we arrived in Gaviota where 101 joined California SR 1, the Pacific Coast Highway.

In Lompoc, we found a coffee shop, and I purchased my usual two-Splenda latte but only after Charlize found a suitable location for a long overdue pee. Since we were in no particular hurry, I occupied a table in the sun outside the coffee shop. Charlize was content to lie in the shade I created. Within minutes, a lady stopped and asked if she could pet Charlize, who is always open to new friendships. It wasn't long before I found out she had two German shepherd dogs who were also rescues.

She noticed the Washington plates on Old Blue, and we were soon in conversation. I found out that her father, in his mid-eighties, lives in Edmonds where she was raised. Her dad recently had a stroke, and she had to move him from his home to a private elder-care home. She said the family that owns the place is very nice, very experienced in caring for the elderly, and her dad has his own little suite in the house. She told me he seems to be happy with his situation, but I had the feeling she was trying to convince herself. After she left us, I turned to Charlize: "You see what we have to look forward to, old girl? Hopefully you won't be around when that happens to me. I need to keep my act together until you are ten or twelve, I suppose."

Charlize looked at me with the quizzical expression she gets when trying to fathom what on earth I'm talking about, and she responded to my voice only with a tail wag. I suppose that is about as much as I can expect for any kind of morbid thinking. She was happy to leap back into Old Blue.

Back on the road, we made our way, twisting and turning, rarely reaching speeds of fifty miles per hour. Most of the time, we had to slow to twenty-five or thirty for the curves. On our left were spectacular ocean vistas, one after another. We found a place for lunch in San Simon, and Charlize made friends with an adorable four-year-old named Matilda, who was sitting with her family at the table next to us on the patio.

Matilda's mother told me it was impossible to keep her away from any dog; she just had to pet all of them. I offered some grandfatherly advice about being too trusting of strange dogs, but it was clear that my warning had little effect on either mother or daughter. One more thing on the long list of things I have no control over. I put Charlize in a "down stay," and she was happy to have Matilda's attention.

It was a spectacular afternoon driving on the coast highway, stopping every half-hour, or so at an overlook just to gaze at the waves coming in and the surf breaking. Eventually we arrived in Monterey. After settling in to the historic Casa Munras Hotel, Charlize strolled alongside while I limped to Cannery Row where Charlize introduced me to more friendly folks. Charlize is impatient and fickle, though. If the conversation lasts more than three or four minutes and nobody is paying sufficient attention to her, she gets anxious to be off to find another new friend.

That evening, Charlize and I ate tapas on the dog-friendly patio at the hotel, and she made friends with all the service staff. I was just along for the experience and to pay the bill.

44

ELEPHANT SEALS AND
AMAZING SCENERY

CHARLIZE AND I STOPPED at yet another vista, this one full of cars, trucks, campers, RVs, and a lot of folks. The signs for the place identified it as Elephant Seal Beach, and the attraction was a lot of elephant seals sunning themselves on the sand and a few frolicking in the water just off shore.

Northern California beach full of elephant seals sunning themselves.

The seals aren't dead but are mostly motionless. Every now and then, one of them digs up some sand with a flipper and flings the grains up into the breeze, covering its body with a thin crust. I have no idea what that accomplishes, maybe the action distracts some biting flies or other pests. I'm certain they wouldn't do it unless it accomplished something, and most of them seem to participate from time to time.

The water was an unbelievable blue, and despite all the people, it was another amazing experience to add to my journal. Many of the folks stopped to chat and pet Charlize. I never cease to be surprised about how easy it is to open a conversation with strangers with my dog as the ice-breaker.

The seals are northern elephant seals, sea mammals that spend from eight to ten months per year out in the open sea. While out and about, so to speak, they are able to dive from a thousand to as much as five thousand feet down searching for a meal. That is an amazing statistic, as any scuba diver will tell you. Each sixty-three feet below the surface of the water is equal to one atmosphere of pressure. That means they can withstand almost eighty atmospheres of pressure, enough to crush almost anything made by man, and they can stay down for as long as two hours. The physiology that allows these amazing animals to accomplish this is much too complicated and difficult to explain here, but it is fantastic!

Only about one out of six of these seals manage to survive to adulthood. The pups, especially, are vulnerable to a variety of predators, including man. They were hunted almost to extinction, their oil being second in quality to only that of the sperm whale. By the early 1970s, there were only about a hundred of these animals breeding on Guadalupe Island off Baja California. Even before the US government managed to do anything, the Mexican government passed laws to protect the remaining animals. Our government, with reasonable functionality, managed to pass the Marine Mammal Protection Act in 1972. By 1999, the total population of these amazing creatures was estimated to be about 150,000 with the Piedras Blancas rookery home to about 18,000. Every now and again we do manage to do something right.

Heading north again, we went past Tomales Bay State Park and any number of small towns with familiar names—Cypress Grove, Ocean Roar, Valley Ford, Bodega Bay, Jenner, all names out of a Steinbeck book perhaps? Then we were on an extremely winding road past the Salt Point State Park Campground where we had spent a night in Frog on our first trip. Eventually, we made it to Gualala and checked into the Whale Watch Inn, a charming place with a charming hostess, and a great view of the water from my room. Charlize was welcomed and allowed to stay in the room with me. We both prefer that!

45

EUREKA

THE WHALE WATCH INN doesn't have a breakfast room. At eight in the morning, according to my Timex, a discrete knock on the door announced my breakfast's arrival at the exact time I had selected the previous evening. I opened the door to find a wicker tray waiting for me. There was a tasty omelet, homemade corn meal muffins, coffee, juice, and fresh fruit. I couldn't eat it all, but Charlize was happy to clean up the omelet and muffins. I polished off the coffee and fresh fruit on my own.

After packing and loading Old Blue, we continued north on Highway 1. I was doing my best to concentrate on the road, rather than the distraction of one magnificent view after another. Less than pacific waves crashed against stark dark rocks sending plumes of white water and spray into the salty air. On the beaches, the waves retrieved grains of sand and carried them back to the ocean floor, only to replace them with the next tide.

Another magnificent view of the Pacific coast.

We stopped to stretch at Manchester State Park where Charlize made friends with blond, sixteen-month-old Chelsea and her proud parents. Chelsea conducted a long conversation with Charlize who was in a "down stay." I had not a clue about the information and/or wisdom being communicated, but Charlize was completely focused and responded to probing fingers and baby pats with licks. I asked Chelsea's parents if they understood anything the little girl was telling Charlize, but they told me my guess was as good as theirs. Charlize was totally engaged but uninterested in sharing any of Chelsea's secrets with me.

We said our goodbyes, Chelsea crying about being separated from her new best friend. Charlize was thankfully content to stay with me. Her loyalty is sometimes incomprehensible.

We meandered on north to Mendocino. I don't know why that small town seemed so familiar—I can't recall ever being there previously—but it is quaint, a throwback to hippie times, mostly old buildings, many of them decorated with street art. I found a coffee shop, of course. After collecting my two-Splenda latte, I had a short conversation about

German shepherd dogs with a couple of seriously unbathed, heavily bearded philosophers who were occupying the sidewalk in front of the shop. Charlize sniffed each of them once and indicated she was ready to leave. I avoided getting close enough to challenge my olfactory senses. I was content to trust her judgment.

Charlize stayed in Old Blue while I took a quick, self-conducted tour of the Mendocino Art Center, followed by a slow drive-through tour of the town. Inside the art center, the volunteer docent on duty indicated there were lots of writers living and working in the area, along with many local visual artists and musicians. I spotted an open real estate office and went in to chat about local housing prices with one of the agents, just curious to see what living in that mecca for artists might cost. Half a million buys a thousand-square-foot, or less, fixer-upper without a clear view of the coastal scenery. I thought California real estate had been hard hit; apparently not in Mendocino.

Back on Highway 1, the road swung east to Drive-Thru Tree Park where the road magically converted to Highway 101. We continued northward, inland from the coast, and experienced several groves of redwoods, including the Richardson Grove State Park and the Humboldt Redwoods State Park. The highway was now identified as the Redwood Highway offering small samples of once many hundreds of square miles of giant redwood forests. Once again, I wished I could have traveled with Jedediah Smith to have been one of the first Americans to experience that time and place. Charlize, Old Blue, and I crossed and recrossed the Eel River continuing north past Humboldt Bay and on into Eureka where we had reservations at the Carter House Inns.

Main building of the Carter House Inn. Charlize and I stayed in an old Victorian house diagonally across the intersection.

We found the place, actually three separate buildings, on the north end of Eureka's Old Town. Our room was on the ground floor of the Victorian Bell Cottage building with a private outside entrance to the room. I was trying for an artistic view of the building, framed by the setting sun; didn't get it. Our room had wood floors, a bathroom with Victorian fixtures, and a large bedroom with Victorian furniture but a comfortable bed. There was an extra charge for Charlize but came with a flannel blanket and a stainless steel food bowl as mementos of our stay.

After dinner, Charlize and I went for a walk past the marina where we encountered a middle-aged man riding a bike outfitted with a single-wheeled trailer, stacked high with his possessions. A pit bull dog was comfortable on top of the collection. We were never closer than twenty yards or so, but Charlize strained against the leash, and the pit bull rose to his feet, both of them with hackles up. I presume both animals were just defending their respective pack leaders. I put Charlize into a "sit stay" and blocked her line of vision to the other dog. I made her pay attention only to me by touching and talking to her whenever she tried to look for the other dog. She calmed, and the bicycle man and his dog pedaled away without incident.

46

A New Kind of Trip

After Charlize and I arrived back in Edmonds and home, it wasn't long until we embarked on another trip, one that required very new and different skills. Both of us needed to be patient and find ways to control the way we handled day-to-day emotions and frustrations.

Over three years ago, the arthritis in my left ankle started to limit my physical activity and ability to get around pain free. Rosalie and I had investigated what could be done. The options, after consulting experts, were to either replace the ankle joint with a prosthetic or fuse the joint. The advice from the most experienced surgeon we could identify was to continue to use the ankle brace I had been using for over a year and add a cane. He told us that when the pain became unbearable I would know it was time to do something.

A little over a year later, about the time we started thinking surgery on the ankle was a viable option, Rosalie was diagnosed with stage-four lung cancer, and everything was put on hold. After she passed, I was incapable of making any kind of decision regarding my own health. This September, I was no longer able to walk Charlize for more than four or five blocks without intense pain. After our morning walk, I had to ice the ankle and rest it for half a day until it was time to take her for another walk. She was good about it, though, somehow sensing about how long I could manage and happy to turn back toward home after a couple of blocks. She started taking care of her business early in the process so as not to prolong my discomfort.

So back to the surgeon and re-evaluation of the ankle. New radiographs and a CT scan showed significant progression of the disease with loss of almost all cartilage in the main joint of the ankle and bone loss of the distal end of the tibia, the long bone of the leg that forms the first portion of the ankle joint. After more research and discussion with the surgeon, we decided the best option was to fuse the joint and not rely on a mechanical device without the same level of success as artificial knee and hip prosthetic joints enjoy.

On October 9, almost three hours of surgery was completed to the satisfaction of the surgeon. After two nights in the hospital, I was home with a cast and facing twelve weeks of recovery with no weight bearing on my left leg.

So this was the new journey Charlize and I shared. We figured out how to cope, and I will share with you the new challenges, the new friends, new helpers and new strengths we discovered on this continuing journey.

47

UNINTENDED CONSEQUENCES

L ATELY I AM BEGINNING TO THINK that Charlize became upset with me. I think she's worried that something I wrote, information I believed would be helpful, was being used for nefarious purposes. Because the reach of the Internet is global, the potential harm is spreading, and she's worried about dogs and cats everywhere.

Antifreeze poisoning is a significant problem in dogs and cats, one of the, if not the most, common causes of animal poisoning. Back in January 31, 2012, I posted an article on my blog entitled, "Why do dogs and cats drink antifreeze and how does it kill them?" My intent was to educate about the lethality of antifreeze, how to keep from exposing your pet, the signs and symptoms of poisoning, what to do if you suspect your pet has been exposed, and the treatment that can only be provided by your veterinarian.

Since that article was published, my website, DocDavesVoice.com has hosted well over thirty-four thousand visits. A small percentage of those visits were from folks who follow my writings, but the vast majority of the visitors reach the site via search engines. I don't know the exact numbers, but a disturbing percentage of those visitors used, and continue to use, search terms such as "how to kill a dog or cat with antifreeze," "how much antifreeze to kill a dog or a cat," "the best way to kill a dog or cat with antifreeze," or similar wordings.

My website provides daily statistics about the articles that were accessed. It is a rare day when the antifreeze article is not the most read, apparently by folks trying to find out how to rid their neighborhood of a pesky dog or cat. Many of the inquiries come from countries with stray or feral dog and cat problems, but it is still disturbing that people are going to the Internet to find out how to poison animals.

So, what to do? I would like to believe that the article has saved some animals from a horrible death. Antifreeze kills by forming crystals in the kidneys that destroys kidney function, not a pleasant death. Quick response and appropriate treatment by a veterinarian is the only way to save an animal thus exposed. However, if the information is perverted and used to poison animals, should I leave it on the site? Mine is not the only site that provides information about antifreeze poisoning.

OK, too heavy? The argument is that free access to information is not and cannot be bad, only the use of that information in a bad way is bad. Of course, Charlize is not really upset with me, especially not with something I wrote. She has yet to read any of my essays, although sometimes I read portions of them to her. When I do, she provides unequivocal support, rather than critique, constructive or otherwise. It would be wonderful if she would provide me with advice about what to do about this.

48
TRUCKS AND CAMPING TRAILERS

CHARLIZE IS A GREAT TRAVEL COMPANION and provider of comfort and attention. I have been searching to discover how to live on my own after so many years of being married to the love of my life. During this past year, I made a lot of choices, some good, some not so good; all were important to the journey.

I thought having a camping trailer while traveling around the country was a great idea. It was something I thought about from time to time over the years, but Rosalie was never interested. We lived in an eight-by-fifty-foot house trailer when first married, and she was not interested in reliving that experience or anything resembling it. Within a few of weeks after her death, I went shopping for a trailer and found one, which I named Frog. During our first trip, it was a fun new experience, but reality started to settle in soon after. Driving on the open road pulling Frog was OK, but extra concentration was needed when parking, driving in inclement weather, especially high winds, or pulling into a crowded gas stations.

Finding a nice RV park to stay in each night was not as straightforward as expected, and it took me about half an hour to set up Frog and about the same amount of time to disconnect and get underway again the next morning. It was also relatively expensive, fifty dollars a night for most of the commercial parks. Then there was the task of emptying the "black water tank," sewage to the uninitiated. The final blow was gas consumption. When pulling Frog, Old Blue was averaging about eight or nine miles to the gallon, and for many of the places we went, gas cost close to or exceeded four dollars a gallon.

Old Blue, a year old when I purchased her, was also a reaction to Rosalie's death. I had been driving a ten-year-old pickup truck, and Rosalie had been driving a van less than two years old. After her death, every time I got into her van, I started to cry. I was already anticipating taking a long road trip with a camping trailer, so I traded her van and my old truck for a year-old, high-end, Dodge Ram 1500 four-door crew-cab with four-wheel drive and over-sized wheels. Old Blue was built for tough, manly activities. I was anxious to get out of our house and separate myself and Charlize from Rosalie's memory and palpable presence in the house. I was not even able to clear out her clothes and other things. I needed to escape all those memories associated with all that physical stuff of hers. So there we were—Charlize, Old Blue, Frog, and I, off to find—what?

49

ANOTHER WAY TO TRAVEL

DURING THE FIRST TRIP Charlize and I took, we wandered for almost six weeks, and I was not yet unhappy with my choices. The second trip we took seemed to involve added hassles with Frog and the RV lifestyle. I began to think that the cost of RV parks and extra fuel might cover the costs of a lot of hotel rooms. Even with the renovations I made to make her more comfortable, Frog was not all that convenient, especially when no utility hook-ups were available. When I left Frog at Don and Susie's ranch or with my son in Carlsbad, I discovered travel was less complicated, less expensive, more relaxing. Gradually I came to the realization that a travel trailer, or any recreational vehicle, was not the choice for me. The idea was reinforced when I found out John Steinbeck spent a lot of time, maybe the majority of his time while traveling with Charley, in high-scale motels and hotels. It was going to be costly, but sometimes one has to admit a mistake, pay the price, and get on with life. So I sold Frog; she was gone. It cost me, but what life lesson doesn't?

Another reality was in store. I really liked Old Blue, but even when not pulling the trailer, gas millage was an issue. On the best of days, on the highway at modest speeds, even with "Eco-Boost," I could only expect sixteen or seventeen miles per gallon. Then there was my garage. After I got her home, I discovered Old Blue was five inches too long to fit into my garage. When trying to park in the parking garage at the Harborview Medical Center or at the building where my lawyer's office was in downtown Seattle, I found that I sometimes had to stop and back up to get around some close corners and into a parking spot without clipping a post or a big car parked in a compact spot.

With the specter of twelve weeks of recovery after my scheduled ankle surgery, not being allowed to bear weight on my left leg for that amount of time, I practiced getting in and out of the truck using just my right foot. I found it all but impossible. Old Blue was just too high off the ground.

So Charlize and I went car shopping. We found a new crossover SUV that was easy for me to get in and out of using just one foot. The sales people at the various automobile dealerships probably thought they we dealing with a weird old man when they observed me testing my ability to ingress and egress from their various models. The new vehicle, actually a computer with four wheels, gets excellent gas millage, has enough room for Charlize, and comes with everything we might need for road trips. It's also easier to keep clean.

Was trading Old Blue for the new car another poor choice, made too quickly? I don't know yet, but I'm glad I'm not struggling to get in and out of Old Blue on one foot, or stuck in the house because I can't. The new car also fits into my garage.

So—the journey continues, life's journey that is. Steinbeck traveled with his dog Charley searching to define the America of that time. My Charlize and I will continue our travels, but my search to find out how to live without Rosalie is resolving. I still miss her every day but am becoming more accustomed to making my own decisions and finding something interesting and worthwhile to accomplish each day. I am more comfortable with the philosophy that each person's life is a journey. Inevitably, we end the journey alone, and along the way have to learn to deal with the loss of loved ones. Both Rosalie and I lost our parents years ago, and we came to accept that as a normal part of the journey. Losing Rosalie was much more difficult but also part of the same journey. Losing a child would be devastating, but many others have coped with even that; I pray I never have to.

Charlize, I realize, has an easier life to deal with. She lives only in the moment. She obviously has memories of some sort of abuse, but they intrude only when something happening in the present brings back those memories, for example when I correct some behavior I don't think appropriate. I wouldn't ever think of hitting her, but someone in her past struck her, based on the way she responds when I raise my voice.

50

STUCK IN THE HOUSE

ONE ASPECT OF GROWING OLD, for animals and us humans, is that joints wear out. Osteoarthritis is characterized by loss and/or degeneration of the cartilage in joints. The process is accompanied by osteophytes that are new bone growth where it is not wanted or needed. These changes are the body's unfortunate, ineffective effort to immobilize the joint and stop continued wear and tear. This is a problem I am quite familiar with having treated many old dogs, cats, and horses trying to alleviate the pain and discomfort associated with the condition. And then I became intimately familiar with it when I had to deal with my ankle.

After the surgery on my ankle, the initial cast was removed two weeks later, and I was fitted with a plastic boot. I got around on crutches and something called a "knee scooter." It is kind of fun to scoot around on this device on a hardwood floor, even carpeting, but stairs and rugs make the trip hazardous. It was also difficult to put the scooter in my vehicle and take it out again while managing crutches and balancing on one leg. I admit to having a problem allowing people to help me, something my sons are constantly giving me grief about. Can't help it; it's the way I am.

I did do one smart thing by hiring a very nice young lady to just be around if I need her. She helped out during the day, walked Charlize, did some chores and errands, and kept me company. An added benefit is her sixteen-month-old daughter. I was, somehow, smart enough to insist that she not pay a babysitter, just bring the baby with her. I relate well to animals, young and old, and to small children, and the little girl is a happy—no, joyous—child who speaks a language that not even her mother understands. She loves Charlize, and Charlize reciprocates. She keeps me smiling whenever she is here with her mother—almost every day. My regular cleaning lady also stepped up to help this old man manage.

The first couple of weeks post-op were not fun with post-op pain masked by the mind-numbing effects of the painkillers prescribed along with all the side effects of those opioids. I was able to stop taking the opioids in just a few days, but the toughest part was sleeping on my back with the leg elevated for the first two or three weeks. What a huge relief to get past that and be able to sleep on my side again!

The next obstacle was getting in and out of the house while nego-tiating the two steps down into the garage. After not being able to get out of the house for several weeks, I was suffering significant cabin fever. Perseverance and practice with the crutches finally paid dividends when I realized I had to trust the crutches to hold me up, balance by holding the bad leg forward, and swing down or up instead of trying to hop. Once out of the house and into my recently purchased vehicle, driving was not a problem since it was my left ankle that had the surgery, the vehicle was purchased because I was able to get in and out using only my right leg, and the car has an automatic transmission, no clutch requiring the use of my left leg. Maneuvering on crutches to be able to get into the vehicle also took practice, but I was free again! I could get to the Corner Coffee Café for my regular fix, take myself on errands, including grocery shopping, a chore I found to be very difficult to assign to others since my habit is to go to the store with a list of things I'm out of but to shop for inspiration of what to prepare for meals.

Throughout this experience, Charlize was both understanding and good. She loved going for her twice-a-day walks with my helper, but I was happy to reclaim that time with her as quickly as I could. When we were alone in the mornings and evenings, she was very attentive and obviously concerned about me. I had long conversations with her about the resumption of our travels. I think she missed the open road as much as I did.

51

SEAMAN

CONFINEMENT WHILE MY SURGICALLY FUSED ANKLE healed provided time for reading, perhaps too much. No—that's not possible. Along with my infatuation with all of Steinbeck and Hemingway, I am addicted, as I've previously mentioned, to any publication that deals with the Corps of Discovery, the Lewis and Clark expedition. I own at least a couple of dozen books dealing with those adventures.

While rereading the three volumes edited by Elliott Coues, I discovered something new to think about. It seems that each time I revisit those accounts of the great adventure I find something I hadn't noticed previously. The history of the Coues edition is interesting in itself. After returning from the mouth of the Columbia River, both Lewis and Clark promised to publish their journals but didn't get around to it. After Lewis's untimely death, Clark traveled to Philadelphia to find an expert to edit and publish the over twenty-seven separate volumes, some only partial journals, that survived the trip. The expert he selected was Nicholas Biddle, who in 1814 published *History of the expedition under the Command of Captains Lewis and Clark, to the sources of the Missouri, thence across the Rocky Mountains and down the Columbia River to the Pacific Ocean*. Snappy title, eh? The book didn't sell well because a member of the corps, Patrick Gass, published his journal of the trip shortly after their return; thus, the basic story was already well known.

Biddle trimmed about two-thirds of the journal entries to create his narrative. Elliot Coues and his "expert copyist" Mary Anderson were granted access to the original journals seventy-eight years later, in 1892. Anderson deciphered misspellings and abbreviations and completed a word-for-word, handwritten transcript. Coues used her transcript to create *The History of the Lewis and Clark Expedition*, first published in 1893. He added many footnotes based on his own travels along the route, Gass's publication, and partial journals from other members of the corps, along with much of the original journal information that was left out by Biddle.

Sorry. Too much information? I warned you that I am an addict. Anyhow, during my latest binge of rereading I rediscovered that in 1803, while in Philadelphia preparing for the journey, under President Jefferson's direction, Lewis purchased a black, male Newfoundland dog, for which he paid twenty dollars. The basic pay for privates in the Corps of Discovery was five dollars a month while Captain Lewis earned forty dollars per month.

Newfoundland dogs are massive. Males can weigh 130 to 150 pounds and stand twenty-two to twenty-eight inches at the shoulder. They have webbed feet and are powerful swimmers, bred to retrieve from strong ocean currents. They also have a thick, oily, waterproof coat. When they swim, they don't dog-paddle; the limbs move up and down in a sort of modified breaststroke.

Lewis's dog was named Seaman, but errors in transcription of the journals identify him as Scannon in many writings about the expedition. He became a favorite of the corps and functioned as a watchdog often warning of danger. Many of the Native Americans the expedition encountered wanted to purchase the dog, but of course, Lewis always refused. One journal entry recounts a time when a deer was wounded by one of the hunters and jumped into the river to escape. Seaman went in after the deer, caught it, drowned it, and retrieved it. He made the entire trip to the Pacific and back, and legend has it that after Lewis committed suicide, or was murdered, at an inn in Tennessee on his way to Washington, Seaman wouldn't leave Lewis's grave and died of starvation guarding his master.

I am still trying to find out how the dog survived the trip from the western slope of the Rockies to the Pacific. At many times during this portion of the trip, the corps faced starvation, sometimes subsisting on rotting dried and pounded salmon and various roots purchased from the Native Americans. This diet, when they could acquire it, made many of them ill. During this period, it is also estimated they ate about three hundred dogs, meat that the Native Americans of the Columbia watershed did not use but that the corps apparently considered acceptable, if not tasty. What did Seaman eat during these times? The issue is not addressed in any of the writings that I can find.

I've discussed this issue with Charlize—what else did we have to talk about during my forced inactivity? She is concerned with the possibility, as I am, that Seaman might have turned cannibal.

52

SEARCHING FOR A MEANINGFUL LIFE

So—PHASE ONE IS COMPLETED, and I'm ready for phase two. I know I can manage life on my own. The next question is what do I want to do with the rest of it? There are many societal issues that demand attention; families who are homeless for whatever cause, health care for all our citizens, equal opportunity, the ongoing fight against any and all kinds of prejudice, responding appropriately to natural disasters, saving Puget Sound, maybe all the oceans … the list is endless. These problems are all so gigantic they become overwhelming. Can one person make a difference? I hope so and am determined to add my voice and support and personal involvement at every opportunity. The first step in any journey is to actually move, commit, do something, anything. Maybe I can even convince others to join in.

We are now in the time of the year when we are inundated with requests for financial support from all manner of worthy organizations, some more worthy than others, some just scams. How to decide? Should I donate enough to one or two, possibly to make a difference, or give a little to as many as possible? If I win the lottery, could I make all of them happy? Not likely. I am determined to try to make a difference.

However, Charlize and I are both ready for the next phase. It is a good thing that she is such a people dog because I am considering dating again.

What are you laughing at Charlize?

Rosalie and I used to tease each other. We would claim the only reasons we stayed together were family, laziness, and the fact that dating would be just awful.

"I cannot imagine you keeping a conversation going and being charming for a whole evening," she would tell me. "How could you possibly date someone?"

"Well, you wouldn't have any trouble talking," I would respond, "but if you didn't feel anything for the person you were out with, could you really continue to be charming?"

"Probably not, not much patience for that," she would laugh. "Guess we'll just have to keep each other."

It was, of course, just teasing. She was always talkative and charming and wouldn't have had any trouble dating at all. She was also much too kind to hurt anyone's feelings. Conversely, I tend to be taciturn and especially bad with chit chat. I can maintain a conversation of substance, if interested in the topic, but cocktail-party conversation eludes me. Rosalie could and often did initiate a conversation and charm complete strangers. I expect I will have to rely on Charlize to break the ice and serve as a subject of conversation.

The good news is that, given the realities of the life insurance actuarial tables, there are significantly more eligible ladies than men out there. The problem is how to meet them.

Rosalie and I didn't realize until the twenty-first century came around that we had a relationship; we just thought we were married. I'm still not certain I am ready for a relationship, however that is defined. Doesn't seem like that much of a challenge, say I, tongue in cheek. I'm relying on Charlize's stamp of approval, of course. Love my dog, love me—or is it vice versa?

53

WHAT THE FUTURE HOLDS?

B OTH SETS OF MY GRANDPARENTS arrived in America at the turn of the twentieth century. They came from Eastern Europe countries where their lives were no longer tenable. After settling here, they faced uncontrolled oscillations in the economy that wiped out small businesses and cut the pay of laborers. Those who worked with their hands, including my paternal grandfather and his brothers, realized they had to unite, so they helped organize labor unions. Big business owners retaliated by hiring professional strikebreakers, scabs. Streets took on the appearance of war zones. The robber barons accumulated even greater wealth and political power and flouted both. Any of this starting to sound familiar?

I never knew my zaydee (grandpa) Gross. He died when I was still an infant. He and his brothers, all carpenters, came from a shtetl, a Jewish ghetto, someplace in Eastern Poland. They were escaping from the most recent attack on Jews in an endless cycle of pogroms. Although the brothers eventually started their own construction company, they remained strong union supporters and progressive thinkers.

My maternal grandfather worked menial jobs long enough to accumulate capital that he then invested into a mind-boggling array of small, usually one-man, businesses that prospered and went broke as each early twentieth century recessionary cycle repeated. After his wholesale produce business in upstate New York folded, he loaded a backpack with sundries—ribbon, thread, needles, pins, that sort of stuff—left his wife and two children with a brother's family, and walked the Erie Canal to Cleveland selling door-to-door along the way. When he reached Cleveland, he had enough capital for three packs. He hired two men to work for him and continued. By 1929, he owned a small department store, and his son, my Uncle Percy, was attending the Ohio State University. Everything was lost, and my uncle left school to join his father collecting junk with a horse and wagon. Before long, they had a truck, then leased some land for a junkyard, and soon after the Second World War started, owned nearly a city block of Solomon and Son Salvage.

When Grandpa Solomon was in his nineties and I was a practicing veterinarian, he sometimes went with me while I made calls to treat horses and other livestock. He would tell me stories about his life as a boy in the Jewish ghetto outside Riga, Latvia, where his father operated a small dairy farm. He recounted home remedies used on his father's one horse and half-dozen milk cows and questioned whether my modern veterinary treatments were as effective. He never learned to read or write English but read the Yiddish newspapers and knew all of Sholem Aleichem's stories. A half-smile wrinkled the sides of his lips and the skin around his eyes when he told me his father could have been Tevye of *Fiddler on the Roof.*

So, my heritage is one of fiscal conservatism, coupled with a strong entrepreneurial bent and a dedication to progressive social responsibility. My parents who were influenced and molded by the Great Depression reinforced this.

Now I worry about the world my granddaughters will live in. The industrial revolution replaced muscle power with machine power. There was strong resistance to the inevitable changes, and there was economic dislocation for many. However, people adapted, society evolved, and a new economic system was created that rewarded creativity and intellectual innovation while harnessing machine power making labor more efficient and more productive. That process is still evolving. But we are on the brink of a new revolution where machine power and artificial intelligence will replace human thinking and at least some innovation. Artificial intelligence and massive computers capable of processing huge amounts of data and devising new solutions to problems are on the near horizon.

Significant change is already upon us. Technology, particularly increasingly efficient computer systems, and the Internet provide service and content that previously came with a price tag, and who amongst us is not tempted to take advantage of free anything?

Technology has already taken a significant toll of the publishing industry. Magazines, newspapers, and books that used to employ journalists, editors, publishers, artists, photographers, and writers are disappearing at an alarming rate. Writers and journalists, who were previously paid for their skills and stories, now blog or contribute to online publications; they have little anticipation or likelihood of being paid for their efforts. Electronic publication, much of it by amateurs with little or no editing and no third-party fact-checking, is so inexpensive to produce and sell that the authors cannot survive on the proceeds. Writing is fast becoming a hobby. Those people selling products and services to writers make more money than do those writers from their writing.

Musicians have also been significantly affected. The product of their imagination, skill, and practice is so easily purloined that to benefit, in any meaningful way, from the sale of their music is unlikely. People previously paid as translators are almost completely out of jobs. Free software, available on the Internet, makes instantaneous translation possible, albeit not always accurate but close enough, and the software is being improved and updated continuously.

Pharmacists will soon be replaced by computer software and robotics that will retrieve and package your prescription with little chance for human error. I recently heard a program on NPR talking about software that can take data from sporting events and from financial transactions and compile appropriate stories, no writer needed. Driverless vehicles will soon be available. We will not need cab or bus drivers or delivery people. Pizza or sushi will be delivered to your door by a drone. Artificial intelligence is already in the works that will replace engineers and software programmers. Take that, you nerds!

Let your imagination run wild. What tasks cannot conceivably be done by smart-enough machines? The challenge is to define where we, or rather our grandchildren, fit into this new automated society. What productive work will they find to do? How will they be remunerated for their work? Will the importance of productive work be replaced by something else in the new society? If so, by what? Maybe there is an underlying message in the popularity of apocalyptic novels, movies, and TV programs. They return us to a society that requires basic survival skills.

Charlize is watching me closely as I read this to her. Her head is cocked to one side, her ears erect, her eyes focused on my face. She does not seem to be as concerned about all this as I am, but she is very attentive.

54

ON THE ROAD AGAIN

THIRTEEN MONTHS AFTER ROSALIE'S DEATH, the family and I ended the official mourning period for her. According to our traditional upbringing, the mourning ended with the service for the unveiling of Rosalie's headstone. During this process, I learned something new. The rabbi told us that Abraham started this tradition when he put up a monument to mark the grave of his beloved Sarah.

Charlize sensed my mood, as always, and along with my two sons and their families, we survived the day and celebrated Rosalie's life at her favorite Chinese restaurant. Two days later, my new vehicle, Whitey—I'm finding it harder to be original with vehicle names—was packed and loaded.

Charlize and I worked our way through early morning Seattle traffic on our way to Enumclaw. We had never been to Enumclaw, and I am all about new roads and new experiences. I intended to cross the Cascades via Crystal Pass. My new GPS directed us around a traffic jam on I-5, and before too long, we were headed east across the plateau, filled with hobby farms, towards Enumclaw. We passed small acreages with horses and an occasional small herd of cattle. I spotted an obviously old, large barn sticking out of the mist, probably part of the original large farm that occupied the location. I presume that original place supported a family prior to being subdivided into plots much too small to serve that function.

Charlize's new habit is to keep me awake and focused on my driving by resting her head on my shoulder as I drive. The GPS was programmed to take us across the mountains to Yakima. It warned us of traffic difficulties, directed us through Enumclaw, but gave no mention of the pass being either open or closed. There was traffic coming towards us, heading west. I concentrated on the dry pavement now winding and climbing east through a rainforest. Moss climbed tree trunks, engulfed downed logs, grasped at young trees, and forced its way toward the light from nurse stumps. We passed a few clear-cut openings as we went up and out of the dense forest into more typical mixes of evergreens and deciduous trees. Now and then, vehicles coming from the east approached us. We stopped in the Village of Greenwater for coffee, but I didn't think to ask if Crystal Pass was open. Surely the GPS would warn me if it was not, and all those vehicles were heading west from someplace.

You guessed correctly. We found snow, then more snow, but Whitey is an all-wheel-drive vehicle, no problem, until we arrived at the barricades across the highway and signs informing that the pass was closed.

I suffered only minimal frustration since time was not an issue on this trip. So back we drove to Enumclaw, north to I-90 and the now not so interesting drive over Snoqualmie Pass. I ate a lunch of Mexican food in Cle Elem and filled the gas tank. The sun was out, but there was lots of snow and slush on the ground.

After Yakima, we headed south, finally back to the plan. Now we were seeing new views and vistas of country not previously traveled. The western slope of the Cascades was covered with snow from the most recent storms, but the road was clear and dry. When evening caught us, we stopped in Goldendale and found a motel that would allow Charlize to stay in the room with me. Two hundred fifty dollars would be tacked to the credit card bill if she made a mess, but my girl would never do such a thing, too much of a lady.

The owner of the motel was an Asian lady and very pleasant. I brought Charlize in with me to show how well behaved she is. I related how Charlize was helping me get through a day at a time as a new widower. The motel owner told me that her husband of forty years died three years ago, leaving her to operate the place. We were soon friends of shared experience. When I checked in, there was one other guest, and the next morning, only two other guests and I were in the place. I hope she gets more business when the weather is not so ugly. The rain all night turned a foot of snow into slush in the parking lot.

55

WINTER ON THE EASTERN SLOPE

CHARLIZE'S COLD NOSE ON MY CHEEK got me up and moving at six o'clock in the morning and at 6:59, Charlize fed and walked, my traveling cup filled with a two-Splenda latte, we were on the road traveling south by southeast through forested lands. Clouds hung on the road in the distance ahead of us, turning to mist as we embraced them, the heavy sky overhead. Then there was an opening, a donut hole in the dark cover, and blue-gray light reflecting off puddles on the pavement rushing past.

There is something about driving back roads and empty highways early in the morning that makes me feel free and righteous, a lightness in the chest akin to watching your offspring win at something you know is important to him or her. Anyone who has experienced that feeling knows what I am talking about.

We arrived at the Columbia River, and Charlize asked to get out to check out the view. She loves the snow.

Charlize sees something of interest on the Columbia River.

We stopped for lunch in Bend, Oregon, at the Big Belly Grill House. Who could possibly pass up a place with that name? I let Charlize out of Whitey for a quick walkabout and then put her back in.

"That's a beautiful dog. Is she friendly?" asked the waitress.

"She's very friendly," I responded, "especially to good-looking women." I'm working at sharpening my repartee.

"Can I pet her then? My name is Leece." She held out her hand.

I took her hand. "Leece, not Lisa or Alicia?" I asked.

"No, L-E-E-C-E, pronounced the way it is spelled. It used to be Lisa, but I changed it."

"OK," I said and let go of her hand but not before she gave mine a squeeze. "I'm Dave."

"Please to meet you, Dave."

"Likewise." Again note the sharp repartee.

It was about one-thirty in the afternoon, and the place was empty except for one other customer. Leece asked him if he needed anything else, and he responded in the negative. She told the cook she would be back in a moment. We went out to Whitey, and I opened the hatchback, telling Charlize to stay. Leece petted Charlize after asking her name. Charlize leaned into her and absorbed the attention. When both had their fill of petting, leaning, touching, and licking, I told Charlize to get back to avoid getting hit by the hatch and closed it.

Charlize being a good girl, staying in Whitey after I told her to do so.

"I was afraid of dogs for a very long time," Leece told me.

"That so? Why was that? Did something bad happen to you?"

"When I was about seven years old, I watched as a Rottweiler attacked my cousin and practically chewed his arm off above the elbow. His mother was a Christian Scientist and refused to take him to a doctor, and he eventually lost the arm."

"That's a horrific story. I can understand why you were afraid of dogs. What happened to change that?"

"Well my second husband had two golden retrievers, and they were very sweet dogs. They were much sweeter than the oaf turned out to be. Leaving those two dogs was much harder than leaving the oaf. Anyhow. I'm now a dog person."

57

OREGON AND BEYOND

CHARLIZE AND I WERE DRIVING through southeastern Oregon and then into California. The winter landscape was much like eastern Washington—rolling hills, windmill farms generating electricity, creeks and washes home to the bare, stark silhouettes of cottonwood trees framed against the winter sky. We drove past cultivated fallow fields, but the rows were cut with the slope, up and down rather than terraced and perpendicular to the slope to conserve the soil.

"Why do they cultivate like this?" I asked Charlize.

She didn't respond, but I saw her perk up her ears in the rear-view mirror. We slowed to twenty-five miles per hour through Moro, Oregon. Proudly emblazoned on the wall outside the high school gym was an announcement that both boys' and girls' teams had won state championships. Even at twenty-five miles per hour, we passed too quickly to note which sports or when the students accomplished those historic achievements.

Moro is obviously an agricultural community, the supply center for a region. Outside of town are sprinkler-irrigated fields, the rolling wheels and attached sections idle, resting for the spring and summer workload of providing essential water to the dark soil. I saw no indication of what is grown.

Before we left, early the following morning, I took this
photo while Charlize took care of her post-prandial business.

At mile marker 231, still following Highway 97 south, the evergreen trees on either side of the highway showed scars of a forest fire.
The charred, blackened trunks of the surviving trees bore witness to the
conflagration, but I spotted only an occasional skeleton tree, a sentinel
poking up into the sky. Judging by the size of the new-growth trees,
the fire must have happened eight or ten years ago. Piles of logs not far
from the road indicated logging activity, but it was not clear to me if
the fire-scarred logs were being harvested for lumber or firewood, and
there was nobody around to ask. We were still about forty miles north
of Klamath Falls.

We stopped in Klamath Falls. Charlize had her walkabout, and I
opted for a slice of apple pie and two cups of coffee. The waitress was
unable to shed any light on the mystery of the piles of logs we had passed.
I was getting tired. I presumed, correctly as it turned out, that the coffee and sugar fix would keep me going for another two or three hours.

It was almost six in the evening when we stopped at the Last Resort
Inn in Adin, California, another motel directly out of the 1950s. The
young female clerk who showed us to our room welcomed Charlize.

She seemed anxious to engage me in conversation, but my answers to her questions were dismissive, and she gave up. I was too tired to relate my story or listen to hers, grumpy after a long day.

There was only one place to eat in Adin. The limited menu was displayed on the wall above the counter where I placed my order for an Ortega burger, onion rings, and a Diet Pepsi. As I supposed, the Ortega burger featured a slice of canned poblano chili pepper wedged between the hamburger meat and the other accouterments; enough said.

Joshua tree photo taken through the driver's side window while whizzing past at sixty-five miles per hour.

Charlize and I were on the road early anticipating a long drive to Las Vegas. We motored through the Modoc Forest with intermittent showers, dark gray skies, mist, and low hanging clouds hugging the trees on either side of the highway. The empty highway twisted and turned, but before too long, we were in Nevada, long, empty high desert valleys separating mountain ranges as we gradually progressed south and east. As we climbed from the desert valley, devoid of interesting vegetation, we reached elevations above six thousand feet and observed Joshua trees scattered occasionally amongst nondescript, ground-hugging brush.

58

Old Stomping Grounds

It was after dark when we finally arrived in Las Vegas. We entered on a freeway I knew nothing about, five or six lanes of rush-hour traffic at sixty-five miles per hour. I had the mistaken idea that I could spot a hotel or there would be a sign for one and I would be able to pull off the freeway and check in. I was quickly relieved of that ridiculous idea as the traffic worsened. I gradually inched our way to the right lane and took the first exit I came to. I proceeded to obstruct traffic for seven or eight blocks looking for a place to pull off the street. I spotted a parking lot and pulled into it. Whitey, Charlize, and I made it, all still whole, amazing! The hometown drivers continued to curse my out-of-state license plates as they drove past, no doubt glad to see me get the hell out of their way.

This time my new GPS came through. I was less than a mile and a half way from a pet-friendly La Quinta Inn. I followed the directions to the front door. As tired and frazzled as I was, I don't know how I would have coped without the technology.

I know for certain I am getting long in the tooth (that's how one guestimates the age of older horses). After two long days of driving and two nights in fifties' motels with less than comfortable beds, my shoulders and back are aching. The spacious La Quinta room, modern with plumbing that functioned as intended and a comfortable king-sized bed, convinced me I was living large.

The folks at the front desk recommend a close-by restaurant, and after a nice steak dinner, I returned to the hotel for a long hot shower, and then I caught up with the Winter Olympics. Charlize wolfed down the steak scraps that I mixed in with her kibble. True to old Vegas tradition, the Las Vegas hotel cost less than either of the previous nights' motels.

We were up early and on the road again by seven thirty. I was anxious to revisit old, familiar places in Arizona. We arrived in Boulder City, Nevada, and followed the signs to Hoover Dam. It will always be Boulder Dam to me. We stopped to gawk, along with a surprising number of tourists. Lake Mead reflected the drought conditions of the southwest. The water level was significantly lower than I remembered.

Charlize does her thing making friends with two young couples.

I said hello to two young couples traveling together. They answered very friendly but spoke what I surmised to be a Balkan language. They had a few words of English, but my zero words in their language made it impossible for me to find out what I am certain was an interesting story. I did understand when they asked for the dog's name and gave it but left out my interesting story of travels inspired by Steinbeck and his Charley, it was too difficult to explain more.

Since Charlize doesn't read, she was unable to follow the directions stenciled onto the wall she jumped onto.

Just above Charlize's rump, two lines are visible on the dam. The top line on the dam is the high watermark for Lake Mead.

It was impossible for me to guess how much water was gone from this reservoir.

Next on the agenda were Oak Creek Canyon and Sedona. The sun was out, and the outside temperature gauge in Whitey read seventy degrees; this was my Arizona in February.

In the late 1940s, my family used to go camping in the Oak Creek Canyon. Sedona then consisted of a gas station and a general store. There might have been a dozen or so rustic cabins sprinkled along the canyon. Progress and population evoked change. The canyon seemed full of inns and restaurants and summer homes all crowding in on the remaining campgrounds. Sedona resembled a huge tourist mall, crowded with cars, RVs, and people.

Note the landscape, the red rock formations poking over the clutter.

I took Charlize for a walk. One of the places we passed advertised "The history of Oak Creek Canyon and Sedona." We did not go in so I have no idea what they were selling, maybe just providing free information, but my impression of today's Sedona was that not much is given away free. There I go again, complaining about progress. But I urge you to imagine what Sedona looked like before this photo.

59

BACK IN ARIZONA

AFTER EATING OVERPRICED MEXICAN FOOD—fancy presentation, ordinary taste—in Sedona, Charlize and I braved the traffic to Cottonwood. The old two-lane road is now a divided highway. The last time I was in this part of the world, there were no divided highways, and Cottonwood was a small village, twenty-odd miles from Sedona on a twisting two-lane road. Another CSU veterinary school graduate, who graduated two or three years behind me, established a practice in Cottonwood in the 1960s. He barely made a living for several years. I lost track of him after leaving Phoenix, but if he stuck it out, it appears plenty of people moved in for him to make a go of it. The whole valley, from Camp Verde to Cottonwood to Clarkdale, is now full of houses, strip malls, big-box stores, and hobby ranches on both sides of Highway 260.

It is only forty-three miles from Clarkdale to Prescott and another fourteen from Prescott to Granite Basin where, in the summers of 1950 through 1952, my dad and I built a cabin in the shadow of Granite Mountain. My brother Joe, three and a half years younger, worked with us, but he claims his only job was to straighten bent nails. I seem to remember him doing a lot more, but he is expert at straightening bent nails.

The view from Jerome, on Cleopatra Hill, looking down into the valley. The cluster of buildings in the left center is Clarkdale. The distant mountains include a portion of the Prescott National Forest, the Tuzigoot National Monument, Dead Horse Ranch State Park, and the Camp Verde Indian Reservation.

We built the cabin on US Forest Service land with what was supposed to be a ninety-nine-year lease. Along the way, a lot of rules got changed. After Dad retired, he and Mom lived in the cabin, except in the winter when they traveled to Guyamas, Mexico, where they parked their travel trailer near the beach. After Dad, died it fell to Joe, living near Cave Creek north of Phoenix, to use and maintain the cabin. It became more and more of a chore as the years passed. For the last few years, every time Joe and his wife went to the cabin, they both had to work at repairing, maintaining, cleaning, and cutting away brush for a fire break. They had to work so hard they usually returned to Phoenix ill. Along with all the labor necessary, insisted upon by the Forest Service, the place was costing thousands of dollars each year. The ground rental increased from thirty-five dollars a year in the 1950s to over two thousand, plus taxes, association dues to maintain the water system and roads, property insurance, and the cost of repairs and maintenance. They finally sold the cabin recently. It is now a place of fond memory, rather than a constant financial drain and worry.

Jerome, Arizona, today.

I have not been back to the cabin since we scattered Mom's ashes there in 2001. I decided to rely on my memory of the good times, rather than revisiting the place. I have it well pictured in my mind, along with a few old snapshots tucked away someplace. I need to find those photos.

Whitey took us up the steep road to Jerome. Back in the day, the family sometimes drove from the cabin through Prescott Valley to Jerome. Then it was a true mining ghost town, full of abandoned houses and buildings just made for us kids to explore and create our own stories and imagined legends. When Charlize and I arrived this time, we found the place full of tourists taking photos of other tourists with their digital cameras. So Charlize and I joined them.

Many if not all the buildings and houses have been resurrected. People have returned to live in Jerome, living off the tourist trade, I presume. All the shops indicate thriving tourism.

Blooming cactus in the Sonoran Desert in February.

We didn't tarry in Jerome. Less than two hours later, we were again near Cave Creek at my brother's house in the desert north of Phoenix. My runny nose and allergy-clogged head reminded me of the almost-forgotten reasons leaving the Valley of the Sun was not difficult.

60

HEADING HOME

WHILE VISITING WITH MY BROTHER and his family in the desert for a couple of weeks, Charlize and I reveled in sun, warm temperatures, and one gully washer consisting of heavy rain and hail. Then we made the now-easy drive to Carlsbad, California, for a visit with my son and his family. More sun and warm temperatures, and Charlize and her pal Bentley were given the opportunity to play in the surf at the dog beach of Delmar.

Charlize focused on the ball, Bentley not so much.

The subdivision where my son's house is located is full of homes with owners who care about and spend time and/or money on their front yards. While walking Charlize one morning, I snapped this photo of a succulent garden next to the sidewalk. It mimics a coral reef, doesn't it? Enough to make a man and his dog smile.

Succulent garden in a Carlsbad, California, subdivision.

After a short week visiting with my granddaughters and their parents, Charlize and I, gone from home for almost a month, were ready to get back on the road. I planned ahead, delaying our departure until late enough in the morning to hit the LA traffic between ten and eleven in the morning. My logical reasoning was that timing our trip in this manner would allow us to hit the freeway at a less crowded time. Wrong! We were stymied by heavy traffic, moving at an average of about ten miles per hour until the five lanes of freeway eventually became a parking lot.

Almost an hour later, we finally cleared the accident. The site was crowded with two fire trucks, two police cruisers, and three wrecked automobiles occupying three lanes. We made it to Paso Robles early enough to spot a Charlize-friendly La Quinta and checked in. That evening, the hotel hosted a free wine-and-cheese tasting with some outstanding Zinfandels that the area full of wineries is known for. Nice!

At the end of the next day, we stopped at another of those fifties' motels, this one in Trinity, California, a beautiful place close to Trinity Lake and on the Trinity River, an area made famous by the gold rush.

Fifties motel in Trinity, California, where Charlize and I stayed.

The next day, we were off early after a stop at a local coffee shop next door to the motel, the real reason I chose that motel. Their doughnuts and sweet rolls were all made on site, fresh, warm, and too delicious for my waistline. The coffee was good too. We left the town shrouded in mist and worked our way to the top of the pass where Charlize discovered fascinating scents that occupied her attention until I finally lost patience.

*Charlize found something of abiding interest along the Trinity River,
here flowing through the memorable landscape.*

We worked our way back to 101 and the Oregon coast, stopping
often just to absorb the endlessly changing scenes of rocks, water, mist,
waves, wildlife, and peace. Good for the soul. We stopped that afternoon
in the little town of Yachats, Oregon, north of Coos Bay and south of
Newport. There are an amazing number of beach homes between the
highway and the sea and numerous small towns to serve the transitory
occupants. It is amazingly beautiful, but I'm not convinced I would
enjoy living that close to neighbors. I didn't bother to inquire about
the cost of that real estate.

The hotel/resort we found in Yachats was right on the cliff next
to the ocean. They welcomed Charlize, and it wasn't that much more
expensive than the motel in Trinity and even had a good restaurant.
My room faced the ocean with a great view, and Charlize and I were
able to take a long walk along the cliffs that evening.

Charlize still didn't read the sign: "unstable cliffs, stay back." Charlize weighs only seventy-five pounds and was quite interested in whatever was happening over the edge. I stayed well away.

The next morning, we continued north along the coast where we encountered more breathtaking scenery but, again, many small towns. Once clear of the towns, we frequently encountered people driving thirty miles per hour in fifty-five-mile-per-hour zones. They were busy taking in the views, but I got impatient. We had been gone from home for nearly five weeks, and I was getting anxious to sleep in my own bed. North of Lincoln City, I spotted Oregon Route 18 angling north and east to Portland. We drove through some interesting rolling hills and farm country, through some Portland suburbs, and hooked up with I-5. The traffic was heavy, requiring hard concentration. I'm not a fan of freeway driving, much preferring the back roads, but I pulled into my driveway before four that afternoon. Home again and glad to have arrived safely!

Epilogue

THE COMEDIAN GEORGE CARLIN did a bit about "stuff." (You can go to YouTube and see it.) Stuff is important—especially *your* stuff. The only reason to have a house, he says, is to have a place to store your stuff. You have to worry about keeping your stuff safe. But that same stuff keeps you from being free. After almost fifty-three years of marriage, Rosalie and I had acquired a lot of stuff, despite our frequent efforts to clean out excess stuff prior to moving—first to Montana, then to Phoenix, then to Mexico and Ohio and Texas and Kentucky and Illinois, and finally Edmonds, Washington.

When I renovated the house we bought in Edmonds prior to our moving in, I responded to Rosalie's mantra: "A house can't have too many closets or space for storage." So I added a lot of closets and a lot of cabinets and, obeying Boyle's law for gases, the volume of our stuff expanded to fill all those closets and cabinets.

The house has about three thousand square feet, much too much space for one person and much too filled with memories—and yes, stuff. I decided my idea of being really free is not to have any more stuff than will fit in my vehicle, including Charlize and her stuff. So, ever since my return from my last trip, I was getting rid of a lot of accumulated stuff, making at least twelve trips to Goodwill with Whitey maximally loaded, as well as delivering of nine boxes full of books to the Friends of the Edmonds Library.

Then these downsizing activities were placed on hold. I wasn't recovering as well from the surgery on my ankle as anticipated. Radiographs and a CT scan showed that one of the screws was fractured and the bone graft wasn't healing as well as it should. So—back for a redo surgery and another six weeks of no weight-bearing, followed by an additional six weeks of gradually increasing the amount of weight on the bad ankle. This time, however, the recovery became more of an adventure.

Charlize and her two buddies, Zsa Zsa and her sister Mimi.

Before leaving on my last trip, I met Alexis, and we went on a few dates. Dating at my stage of life is just weird! While Charlize and I were on the road again, Alexis and I communicated frequently by email and cell phone. When I returned, we embarked on a more serious relationship. Alexis is bright, very bright, statuesque, fun to be with, independent, intellectual—and we continue to identify more and more common interests and attitudes. When I told her that I had to go back for more surgery and probably at least twelve weeks of recuperation, she gave me my walking orders: "Well then, you're moving in with me so I can take care of you and Charlize while you recuperate."

Alexis has two Yorkshire terriers, sisters but not littermates. The very first time the three dogs met they connected. The two tiny ones love Charlize, and Charlize reciprocates. The three of them invent games to play, usually involving keep-away with stuffed toys that end up eviscerated. When Charlize stretches out on the floor, Mimi and Zsa Zsa climb all over her. She loves it. While I was still using crutches and a knee scooter to get around, Alexis fed the dogs. Charlize is now her new best friend.

Appendix

The Branding—

A Sense of Community

Charlize and I returned to Pass Ranch to participate in the branding of cattle, a culture of community building. No doubt there are more efficient ways of handling cows and separating them from their calves, but with moderate improvements over time, the old ways still provide something more for the families and friends and colleagues who show up to help their neighbors.

My rancher friend Don is gruff. His dad was gruff, and I imagine that his grandfather and great-grandfather were cut from the same tough rawhide.

"We do it the old-fashioned way," he told me. "Over the years, we've made some improvements. The portable pipe corral segments that fit together work. The propane-fired branding iron heater works. The important thing is that the neighbors and their hired hands and all the kids like the cowboy stuff, and this is their chance to experience that."

At six-thirty in the morning, we were sitting at the large kitchen table, drinking coffee and solving the world's problems, Charlize attentive as always, listening to the two old guys. Her head was cocked to one side, trying her best to understand her role in the conversation and that day's coming activities.

While thus occupied, we were looking out of the south-facing wall of windows as truck after truck drove past all hauling goose-neck stock trailers with from two to six horses already saddled inside. "No rush," Don said. "They'll have to gather the first group of cows and calves, get them penned, and the cows cut out before we get started. My guys know what to do."

"It's probably best to leave Charlize here this morning," I offered. "Don't want her getting underfoot or causing problems."

Don glanced at me and the corners of his mouth twisted into something resembling a half-smile. We often think along parallel lines, and he no doubt had been musing about how to broach this subject tactfully. "Good idea."

We drove about five miles west and south of the house to a fence corner where three pastures converged. A temporary set of pens and corrals had been set up using panels made from steel pipe.

The plastic paddles on the end of wood poles are another innovation. They're used to touch the calves on the face to force them back from the opening. The other folks in the corral were actually helping to keep the cattle bunched up, not just standing around for no purpose.

The mounted hands were ready to rope any calf that sneaked through and tried to join the cows. It's one of the fun cowboy parts of the deal.

After the calves are separated, the real fun begins: One of the hands ropes a calf by the hind legs and then drags it to one of two groups of catchers, who are ready and waiting only ten to twenty yards away.

Each group of catchers has two individuals. One of them grabs the rope, pulling the calf by its hind legs. The other team member grabs the front legs, and they lay the calf on its right side, stretching it out, and remove the rope. This is now a unisex activity, changed from the old days. Everyone pitches in, doing equal work. Many of the girls are as skilled as the men and boys at handling the calves and roping. Without any orders, the participants rotate so everyone has a chance to do all of the jobs. At least three or four generations, including children, of family, friends, neighbors, and hired ranch hands all work together to learn a set of skills not easily mastered.

Calves being separated out from the herd, encouraged not to follow the cow.

The downstream side of the previous photo.

The male calves are efficiently and quickly castrated, all calves are vaccinated with two different vaccines, and all are branded before they are released. Theft of cattle—rustling—is still a problem for these ranchers, and a well-branded animal is the best prevention. Hot branding is the fastest, most secure and durable method. Most calves were stretched out only a few minutes.

A just-released little guy looking for his mama.

When we were about three-fourths through with the first group of two hundred-plus calves, a group of riders set out to round up and bring in the second group of cows and calves from an adjacent six-hundred-plus-acre pasture. By the time the last calf of the first group was finished, the second group was already being herded towards the pens.

The first calf was branded about eight thirty that morning. At eleven thirty, more than 550 calves had been handled. At one o'clock that afternoon, all the participants were sitting around card tables on Don and Susie's lawn waiting for the dinner bell to ring. A few were sipping cold beers, but most were drinking soft drinks or iced-tea. All the horses had been cared for and were waiting patiently in their trailers for the ride home. Charlize made the rounds, introducing herself and smelling all the wonderful aromas emanating from grimy jeans, boots, and chaps.

At two thirty, almost everyone was gone, with work waiting for him or her at home. During branding season, two to four brandings a week are scheduled. The ranchers, their families, and their helpers show up and work hard. They are fed well for their hard work but, most important, neighbors and friends gather to do a job that is accomplished best and most efficiently by a large group of folks who know what to do and how to do it while also teaching the young. Damn few things happen that way in our modern society, but the Sandhills ranchers have figured it out and keep it going. I'm sure glad!